YOU ARE CREATED FOR GOOD WORKS

Hear God Calling | Maximize Your Career | Get The Right Job

Name: _____

Email: _____

Phone: _____

© 2020 Crossroads Career® Services, Inc. All Rights Reserved. Please do not reproduce, except for personal use. Crossroads Career® Workbook © Copyright 2000-2020 by Crossroads Career® Services, Inc.

You are Created for Good Works
Hear God Calling | Maximize Your Career | Get the Right Job
ISBN 978-0-9898995-6-7

Published by Crossroads Career Services, Inc.

Printed in the United States of America

"Scripture quotations taken from the New American Standard Bible® (NASB), Copyright © 1960, 1962, 1963, 1968, 1971, 1972, 1973, 1975, 1977, 1995 by The Lockman Foundation Used by permission. www.Lockman.org"

Scripture quotations marked (NIV) are taken from the Holy Bible, New International Version®, NIV®. Copyright © 1973, 1978, 1984, 2011 by Biblica, Inc.™ Used by permission of Zondervan. All rights reserved worldwide. www.zondervan.com The "NIV" and "New International Version" are trademarks registered in the United States Patent and Trademark Office by Biblica, Inc.™

Scripture quotations marked (NLT) are taken from the Holy Bible, New Living Translation, copyright ©1996, 2004, 2015 by Tyndale House Foundation. Used by permission of Tyndale House Publishers, Inc., Carol Stream, Illinois 60188. All rights reserved.

Scripture quotations marked (GNT) are from the Good News Translation in Today's English Version- Second Edition Copyright © 1992 by American Bible Society. Used by Permission.

Scripture quotations marked CSB®, are taken from the Christian Standard Bible®, Copyright © 2017 by Holman Bible Publishers. Used by permission. Christian Standard Bible®, and CSB® are federally registered trademarks of Holman Bible Publishers.

ADOBE STOCK CREDIT
Photographs & images in this workbook are protected by copyright law. Resale or use of any images used in this workbook are prohibited. Images © / Adobe Stock

About Crossroads Career Services, Inc.

God birthed Crossroads Career Services, Inc. on October 19, 1987 in Atlanta, GA as a ministry to help employers and candidates find one another. With the assistance of the Fellowship of Companies for Christ, three people were brought together to lead the new enterprise:

- Betsy McCall, owner of Crossroads Consultants human resources services.
- Whit Blakeley, owner of Atlanta Outplacement Counseling Center.
- Brian Ray, former Chick-fil-A executive and owner of Primus Consulting.

During the first few years, the ministry shifted from staffing for employers to coaching for candidates. As the ministry grew into the 1990s, workshops were offered to small groups and large conferences in churches. As the year 2000 arrived, God blessed the ministry with new vision and provision that included our 501(c)3 status, raising up of a network of churches with career ministry and hiring our first team of executives to lead the nonprofit.

Another round of blessings began in 2010 with strategic partnerships both with The Job Connection and the U.S. Department of Labor. We took our resources to the world wide web and were able to offer them at no cost including free job postings, resume builder, a prayer network and more. Finally, a textbook for pastors and ministry leaders was released entitled, Created for Good Works.

Now, in 2020, we look to grow our reach and impact. With many new board members, expanded technology and strong partnerships with ministry leaders, Crossroads Career is poised and positioned to reach the next 50,000+ people at a crossroads in their careers.

In this next decade we look to expand our overall reach, help those in our influence and build ministry sustainability. We will do that through the equipping of ministry partners, encouraging volunteer growth, establishing metro area leaders and extending ministry to donors, strategic partners and employers.

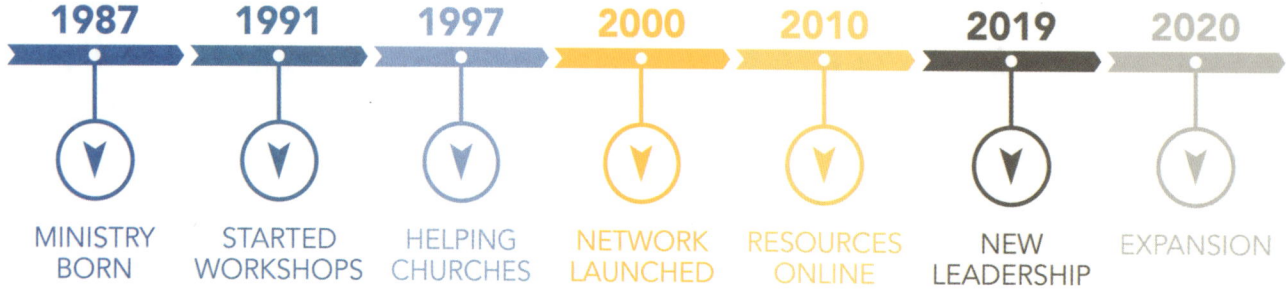

Our Prayer for You

We thank God for you as His masterpiece created for good works. We pray for your journey through this workbook and website to enlighten the eyes of your heart. May you fully receive our Creator's encouragement, comfort, wisdom and joy. We pray the Holy Spirit guides you every step of the way to hear God calling, maximize your career and get the right job. In Jesus name, Amen!

Author Brian C. Ray has been writing, speaking and connecting people to Christ in the workplace for 45 years. He is Co-Founder of Crossroads Career Services, former Chick-fil-A restaurants VP for Human Resources and Administration, and Owner of Primus Consulting, an executive search firm. He has authored Christian resources including *Mastery of Leadership*, *Real Success at Work*, and *New Job Jump Start*. Brian and his wife Kristy live in the Charlotte, NC area.

Editor Brian Horvath is the Crossroads Career Metro Leader in Tampa, St. Pete and Clearwater. He is also President/CEO of The Horvath Training Institute helping people to know, live, and love the purpose for their career and finances. Previously, Brian served ten years at Grace Family Church as Founder and Director of Finance and Career ministries where he led 100+ volunteers to serve 4,000+ people. Brian enjoys sharing life with his wife, Becky, and two children.

WELCOME

**Are you unemployed or underemployed?
Misemployed or miserably employed?
Happily employed, but working without purpose or meaning?**

Since 1987, Crossroads Career Services, Inc. has been helping people walk through crossroads in their careers, based on the truth in God's word.

> For we are God's masterpiece. He has created us anew in Christ Jesus, so we can do the good things he planned for us long ago.
> Ephesians 2:10 NLT

How to work the workbook

This icon indicates a key scripture that we want you to read and reflect upon.

This pencil icon indicates a time for you to write down your thoughts and answers.

This icon indicates a website address that provides important information and downloadable PDF's.

How to work the website: crossroadscareer.org

Join over 50,000 people already registered on our website. You can Register/login for free at crossroadscareer.org to search our Job Connector with thousands of employer-posted jobs, plus you can:

- Set up emailed job alerts.
- Apply for jobs and track applications.
- Create, keep, post and send resumes and cover letters.
- Use the Interest Profiler and Skill Matcher assessments.
- Access our 7-step action plan, career and job resources.
- Post, pray, and praise on our confidential Prayer Network.

YOU ARE CREATED FOR GOOD WORKS
Hear God Calling | Maximize Your Career | Get The Right Job

THE CROSSROADS	1
UPWARD	
Step 1 Upward: Hear God Calling	9
INWARD: MAXIMIZE YOUR CAREER	
Step 2 Attitude: Reach Forward	23
Step 3 Aptitude: Discover Your Best	35
Step 4 Altitude: Target Opportunities	47
OUTWARD: GET THE RIGHT JOB	
Step 5 Searching: Seek to Serve	65
Step 6 Sorting: Wow Interviewers	83
Step 7 Selecting: Walk in Good Works	103

THE CROSSROADS

THE CROSSROADS

Stand at the crossroads and look; ask for the ancient paths, ask where the good way is, and walk in it, and you will find rest for your souls...

Jeremiah 6:16 NIV

At a crossroads in your career?

More than 150 million workers in America face crossroads in their careers every year. About half are dissatisfied with their jobs. Two-thirds are not engaged at work. Millions are unemployed. How about you?

Is Your Job Fulfilling?

National surveys report that about half of Americans are not satisfied with their jobs. How about you? Take a look at the following lists of work situations, and circle those that best describe you.

Unemployed or underemployed?

- Quit, laid off or fired
- Recently divorced or separated
- Retired but need the money
- Relocated to a new area
- Newly graduated from school
- Part-time/need more money after raising children
- Completed military service

Misemployed or miserably employed?

- Stressed out
- Worried about job loss
- Actively disengaged at work
- Need or want to work from home
- Too much time on the road
- Want to be self-employed
- Boss behaving badly
- Don't like or not good at the job
- Unengaged, bored or in a rut
- Too many hours – too little money
- Maybe own your own business
- Have no purpose or meaning

Happily-employed, but?

- Lack sense of purpose and meaning
- Halfway through life wondering what's next
- God is calling you to something else
- Vanity of vanities

Called and Fulfilled?

- Using God-given gifts: experiences, abilities and personality
- Living on purpose. Hearing and following God's calling
- Loving Mondays. Passionate about your work

Make Bad Work Better

Whatever you do, do your work heartily, as for the Lord rather than for men, knowing that from the Lord you will receive the reward of the inheritance. It is the Lord Christ whom you serve.
Colossians 3:23-24 NASB

If you are experiencing anything less than being fulfilled and fruitful in your work, you might be contributing to the problem without even realizing it. If you are doing less than your best, you are short-changing yourself, your employer and God. If you have a bad attitude about your work, boss, coworkers or any other aspect of work, your attitude will hurt your performance and relationships. Ask yourself – are you working heartily as for the Lord?

You might be thinking "Yeah, but you do not know my boss!" You are right, but consider this thought about bosses both good and bad…

 …submit yourselves to your masters, not only to those who are good and considerate, but also to those who are harsh.

1 Peter 2:18 NASB

If "harsh" describes your boss, it is especially important to take your attitude, motivation and performance to their most positive highest. You may be ready to belt, bolt or blow off your boss, but hang in there. You may not know the pressure your boss is under either at work or home. For your own good – now and in the future – take a deep breath, put on a bigger smile and help your boss succeed.

7 Steps To Rocket Your Career

Walking through crossroads is not necessarily about changing jobs or careers. It is always about you being transformed into the person God has made you to be – His masterpiece created for good works that He prepared for you. You can employ this 7-step action plan in order 1-7, or you can select any of the 7 steps based on your highest felt need right now.

Notice in the rocket-like diagram that **Step 1 Upward** is foundational for helping you hear God calling.

Step 2 Attitude and **Step 3 Aptitude** provide movement and direction to give your career **Step 4 Altitude**...

...which leads to **Steps 5-6-7 Searching, Sorting and Selecting** the right job.

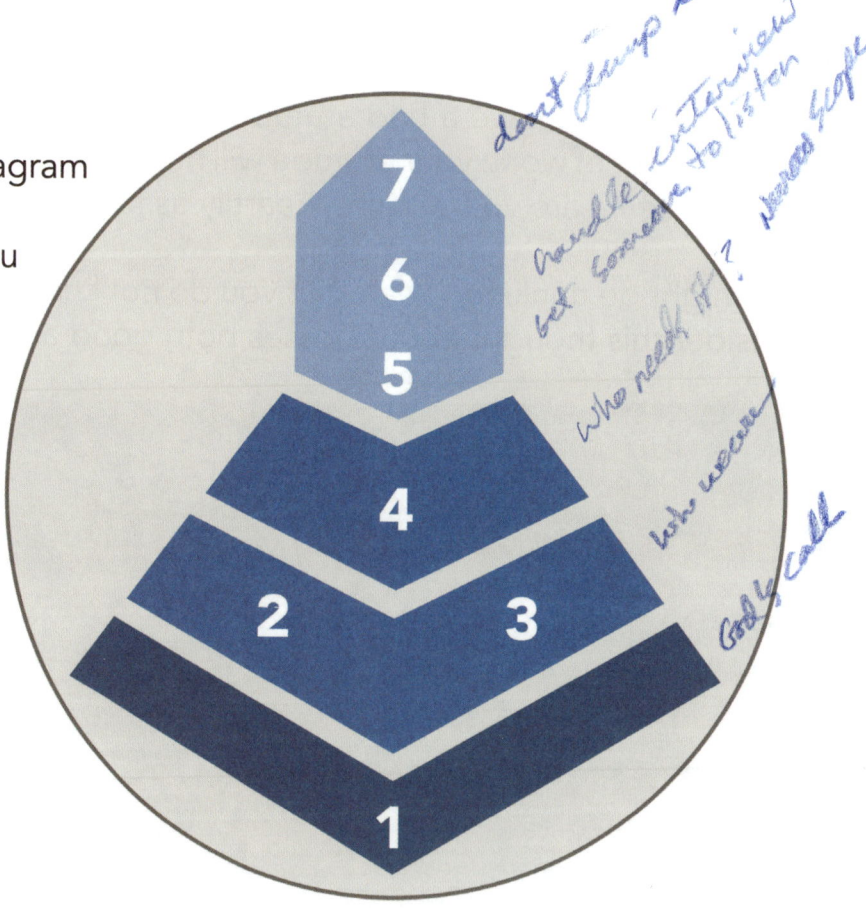

TODAY I AM AT STEP _____

5 The Crossroads

Crossroads Career Groups

Thousands of people have attended Crossroads Career groups online and in person.

Capture your group meeting information below.

✏️ Meeting Information

Dates/Day of Week _____ Time from _____ to _____

Contact Info _____

_____

Leader/Coach _____

Email _____ Phone _____

Also, to get the most of your group, build relationships with your group leader and fellow group members. Connect with them early and often to maximize the group experience.

✏️	Name	Phone	Email

Together Everyone Achieves More

…let us consider how to stimulate one another to love and good deeds… encouraging one another; all the more… Hebrews 10:24-25 NASB

Teamwork makes the dream work. This workbook and our website get exponentially better when you team-up with others, whether online or in person.

GOOD in a workshop → **BETTER** with a buddy/coach → **BEST** in a small group

Find workshops, groups and coaches at **crossroadscareer.org/locations**. The accountability, belonging and care with others multiplies wisdom and strength.

Try these tips for meetings:

1. Attend all meetings.
2. Do your homework before meetings.
3. Explore career resources on our website for each step.
4. Bring your workbook and a Bible to every meeting.
5. Arrive early and stay late for relationship building and networking.
6. Stay in touch with others between meetings by email, phone or text.
7. Pay attention to the leader/coach, as well as your teammates.
8. If you have concerns or critiques, please share with the coach/leader.
9. Maintain confidentiality.

Find workshops, groups and coaches at **crossroadscareer.org/locations**

UPWARD

LOVE GOD COMPLETELY

HEAR GOD CALLING

STEP ONE
UPWARD

"For I know the plans I have for you," declares the Lord, "plans to prosper you and not to harm you, plans to give you hope and a future. Then you will call on me and come and pray to me, and I will listen to you. You will seek me and find me when you seek me with all your heart."

Jeremiah 29:11-13 NIV

Hear God Calling

God knows everyone and everything everywhere, including you, your past, your present, and His plans for your work and for your future. If you have questions and concerns, ask Him. He loves you.

Step One Upward 10

Your Hope & Future

Realize that you are God's masterpiece – body, soul and spirit. Imagine your future not only maximizing your career, but also experiencing a sense of purpose and well-being. Consider your current situation in light of life's five highest felt needs…

What the whole world wants is a good job. When you don't have the right work, nothing works. Even people who climb the ladder of success find disappointment because their ladder might be leaning against the wrong wall.

Instead, ask God about His plans for your hope and future. Set life goals that align with your best understanding of His purposes for you in your current situation.

Write your **LIFE** hopes for yourself, family, friends, health, wealth and work.

Live In Faith Everyday

Write Your Life Hopes

Get help at *crossroadscareer.org/goalsetting*

Step One Upward 12

Work as Worship

When Jesus was asked about the rules for relating to God, He replied with two great commandments.

Love the Lord your God with all your heart and with all your soul and with all your mind. This is the first and greatest commandment. And the second is like it: Love your neighbor as yourself.
Matthew 22:37-39 NIV

Did you notice the command to love yourself in the midst of loving God and others? Starting with the fact that God loves us first, theologian and author Ken Boa describes the flow of love this way:

"When you love God more completely, you see yourself more correctly, as His masterpiece created for good works. When you see yourself correctly, then you are free to love others compassionately."

UPWARD
Love God
completely

INWARD
Love yourself
correctly

OUTWARD
Love others
compassionately

Now is your opportunity to start living out your faith at work. You are not too young, not too old. It is not too late. You are not stuck in the muck. You can survive and thrive. Crossroads in your career are opportunities that bring out the best in you and the best for you.

Learn about work as worship at **crossroadscareer.org/workasworship**

God Is Calling You

The One Who created the world, and everything in it, wants to have a personal relationship with you. He made it possible through His Son Jesus Christ paying the price of death for your sin, the only thing that separates you from Him.

For God so loved the world that he gave His only begotten Son, that whoever believes in Him shall not perish, but have eternal life.

John 3:16 NASB

By accepting this truth, you can have a relationship with the Creator of the universe – Father, Son and Holy Spirit – starting right now and lasting forever. To hear God calling, and follow Him in a personal relationship, consider praying this prayer:

"Dear God, I know I am a sinner, and I ask your forgiveness. I believe Jesus Christ is Your Son. I believe He died for my sin and that you raised Him to life. I want to trust Him as my Savior and follow Him as my Lord, from this day forward. Guide my life and help me to do your will. I pray this in the name of Jesus. Amen"

When you pray this prayer:

- Tell your family and friends who love and care for you.
- Seek people who believe what you just prayed.
- Join a fellowship and a church that teaches, preaches and lives out your new inward commitment.
- Make it habit to pray and read Scriptural devotionals at the beginning and/or end of every day.

Go with God

Imagine getting up every day with the conviction that you are on the planet for a purpose. How fulfilled would you be to know that you and your work matter to God and that He is pleased? How, you ask? Over the past 30 years of helping thousands of people, we have found 11 ways that help people hear God calling and follow His leading.

Circle the ways you daily or weekly seek to hear God calling.

1. **Worship God**
   There is no calling without The Caller. Take dedicated time to praise and thank Him. Then as you live and work every day, do everything to glorify Him. *Ascribe to the Lord the glory due His name; worship…in the splendor of His holiness. Psalm 29:2 NIV*

2. **Study the Bible**
   The Bible is God's written authority and our manual for living. Consider it like bread, and feed on it every day. If the Bible is new to you, start with the book of Psalms, John or Ephesians. *Your word is a lamp for my feet, a light on my path. Psalm 119:105 NIV*

3. **Pray**
   Be in conversation with God every day. You can even confidentially pray with others online at crossroadscareer.org/prayer. Start with a prayer for guidance from *Psalm 143:8 NIV*: *Show me the way I should go, for to you I entrust my life.*

4. **Listen to God**
   Prayer is two-way communication. In a journal, notebook or this workbook, write thoughts that come to your mind. *Be still and know that I am God. Psalm 46:10 NIV*

5. **Fellowship**
   Spend time with Christians who are like-minded and like-valued. Study the Bible and pray together. Encourage one another. Follow the ABCs of Accountability, Belonging and Care. *And let us consider how to stimulate one another to love and good deeds…Hebrews 10:24 NASB*

6. **Seek Wise Counsel**
Seek first wisdom from above (see *James 3:17*) and then from people. Some may be friends. Others might be strangers. All should be of good reputation. *Let the wise listen and add to their learning, and let the discerning get guidance. Proverbs 1:5 NIV*

7. **Consider Your Circumstances**
Be a good steward of opportunities God gives you. Consider unfolding circumstances in prayer, with counsel and in light of the truth of the Bible. *Be very careful, then, how you live…making the most of every opportunity. Ephesians 5:15-16 NIV*

8. **Confess to Clear Your Head**
It is easy to get confused when sin is getting in your way. Confess and clear your mind every day. *If we confess our sins, He is faithful and righteous to forgive us our sins and to cleanse us from all unrighteousness. 1 John 1:9 NASB*

9. **Receive God's Peace**
As you consider various choices, be alert for the peace of God, even in the midst of the most chaotic of times. *And the peace of God, which transcends all understanding, will guard your hearts and your minds, in Christ Jesus. Philippians 4:7 NIV*

10. **Keep a Journal**
Keep track of thoughts you have during Bible study, prayer, fellowship, counsel, confession and unfolding circumstances. *Thus says the Lord, the God of Israel, "Write all the words which I have spoken to you in a book." Jeremiah 30:2 NASB*

11. **Trust & Obey**
There is no other way! If you hear Him, follow Him. *Whoever has my commands and keeps them is the one who loves me. The one who loves me will be loved by my Father, and I too will love them and show myself to them. John 14:21 NIV*

Career x Calling = Maximizing

CAREER, according to dictionary.com, means "an occupation or profession, especially one requiring special training, followed as one's lifework."

CALLING comes from the Greek word KALEO, which means "to call, invite, summon." It refers to a personal relationship with God and the good works He has prepared for you.

Based on the definitions above, what are the differences and similarities between career and calling? Write your thoughts below…

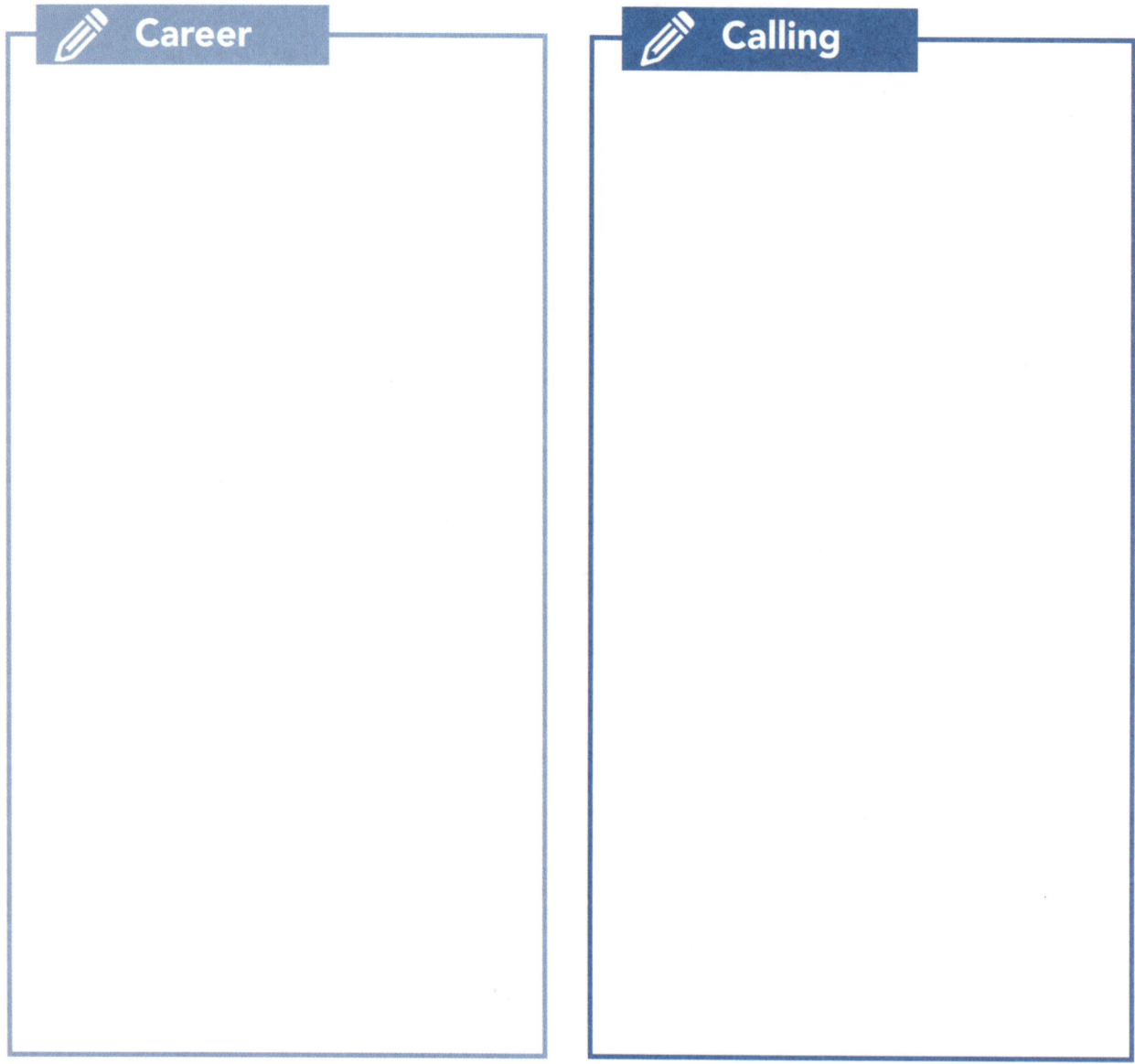

Invest in You

You are your most important asset. Be a good steward of your time, money and effort.

Time
If you are unemployed, invest 40 hours a week. If you are employed, invest 7 hours a week. Commitment and smart planning are required. Finding the right work **is** work.

How long to find a job? Tough question to answer, because it depends on your sense of urgency, how many hours you invest, what job you are seeking, your search plan and how you execute it. The average length of unemployment is six months, according to the U.S. Bureau of Labor Statistics.

How long to change careers? It might take a few days to a few years. The more education and experience you need, the longer it will take. The key is to start now by discovering your strengths and targeting employers that need them most.

Money
In light of how much money you want to make, answer the question, "How much can I invest?" Plan a budget considering these expenses.

- Education, skills training, certifications
- Phone, laptop, tablet, internet
- Career books, directories, publications
- Career assessments, workshops, coaching
- Association memberships and meetings
- Resumes, business cards, postage
- Local and possibly long-distance travel and meals
- New clothes and grooming

Estimated Investment
Whatever amount you decide, set aside the money and invest it wisely. Keep good records. Costs related to job search can be tax deductible. Check with the IRS or your tax preparer.

Effort
Work the workbook. Read every page. Complete every exercise. Read and write every devotional. Register for free on crossroadscareer.org and use our job postings, confidential prayer network, interest profiler, resume builder and 100 more 7-step career resources. Review and preview your progress every week using SMART goals.

Review & Preview Weekly Progress

Power forward every week. Review and Preview every Saturday-Sunday using SMART goals.

Specific: Set weekly goals that are measurable. Define what you want to accomplish.
Moderate: Select 2-5 goals per week. Too many goals can be overwhelming.
Accountability: Show and tell someone what you plan to do. Connect every week.
Record: It is helpful and motivating to keep a written record of progress every day.
Time-activated: Put your plans in your calendar for every day.

List and celebrate progress, accomplishments, blessings. Praise God from Whom all blessings flow. Share with others as appropriate and opportunity provides.

1. _____
2. _____
3. _____

What Did You Learn?

List SMART goals for next week. Don't be anxious!
Be prayerful and include God in your goals for this week.

1. _____
2. _____
3. _____

What Help Do You Need?

Download this weekly exercise from **crossroadscareer.org/progress**

KEY TAKEAWAYS

What did you learn that was most important to you in this step?

Got questions or need help? Explore more Step 1 Resources online

crossroadscareer.org/step-1

*This page is intentionally left blank, feel free to use this area for notes.

INWARD

LOVE
YOURSELF CORRECTLY

MAXIMIZE YOUR CAREER

STEP TWO
ATTITUDE

Consider it pure joy…whenever you face trials of many kinds, because you know that the testing of your faith produces perseverance. Let perseverance finish its work so that you may be mature and complete, not lacking anything.

James 1:2-4 NIV

Reach Forward

Most people enter a crossroads with a mixture of positive and negative feelings...

- **Unemployed?** Are you angry, fearful and depressed or positive with renewed motivation?
- **Misemployed?** Are you miserable in your job, or are you filled with hope for something new?
- **Unfulfilled?** Happily-employed but no purpose? Do you feel empty, or are you exploring new meaning?

As you think, so you shall be.

- "Most folks are about as happy as they make up their minds to be," said Abraham Lincoln, 16th President of the United States.
- "85% of the reason people get jobs and get ahead in those jobs is because of attitude," wrote motivational speaker and author Zig Ziglar.

Think about and pray through this verse from Philippians 4:8 NIV:

Finally, brothers and sisters, whatever is true, whatever is noble, whatever is right, whatever is pure, whatever is lovely, whatever is admirable—if anything is excellent or praiseworthy—think about such things.

Attitude Meter

How do you rate your attitude? Good 7-10, Bad 3-7, or Ugly 0-3? Circle a number in the Attitude Meter that best represents your emotions right now.

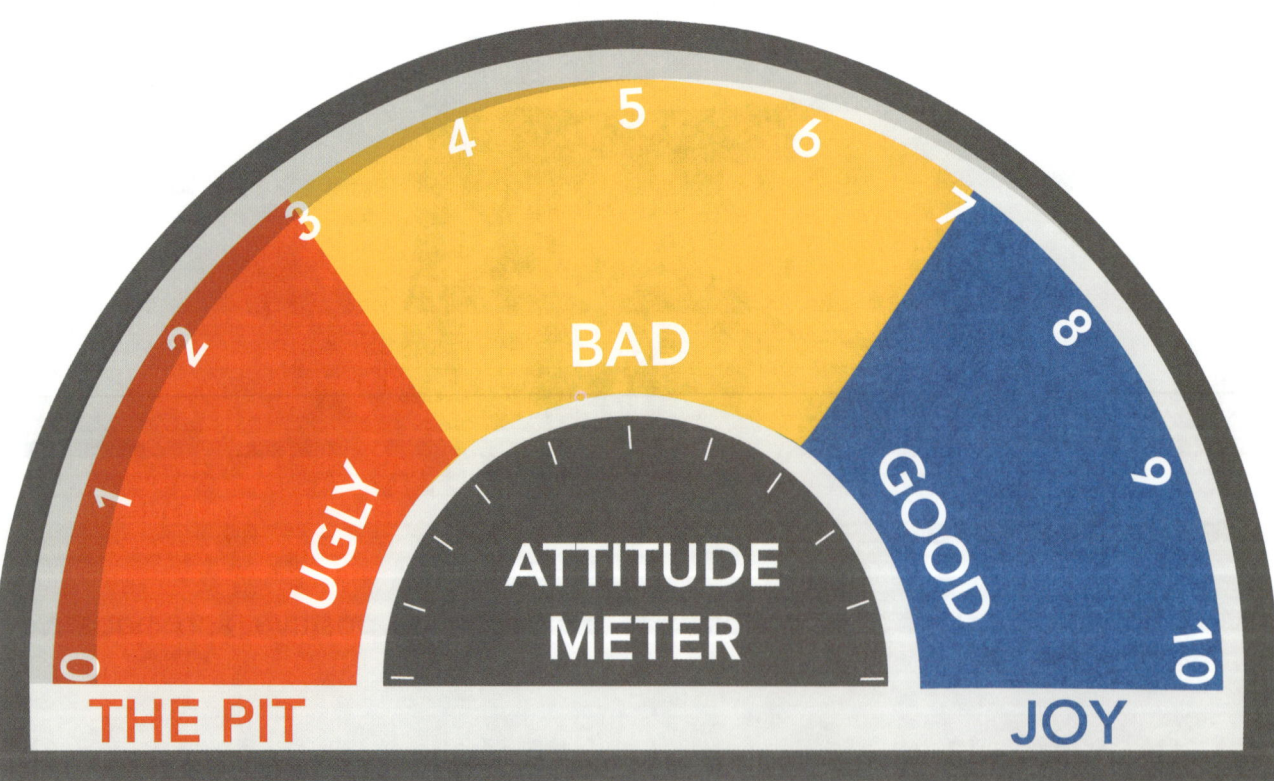

Does your attitude reflect your circumstances? Do bad situations breed negative feelings? Is it possible to be in the PIT, yet live each day with joy? "Impossible," you say?

All things are "Him-Possible" to those who live and love upward, inward and outward. Start with the decision to reset your attitude number. Go to the Attitude Meter draw a box around a higher number.

Briefly Describe Your Circumstances

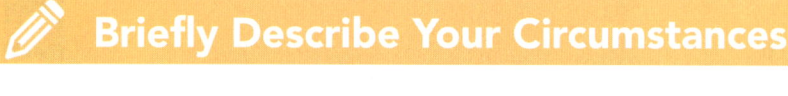

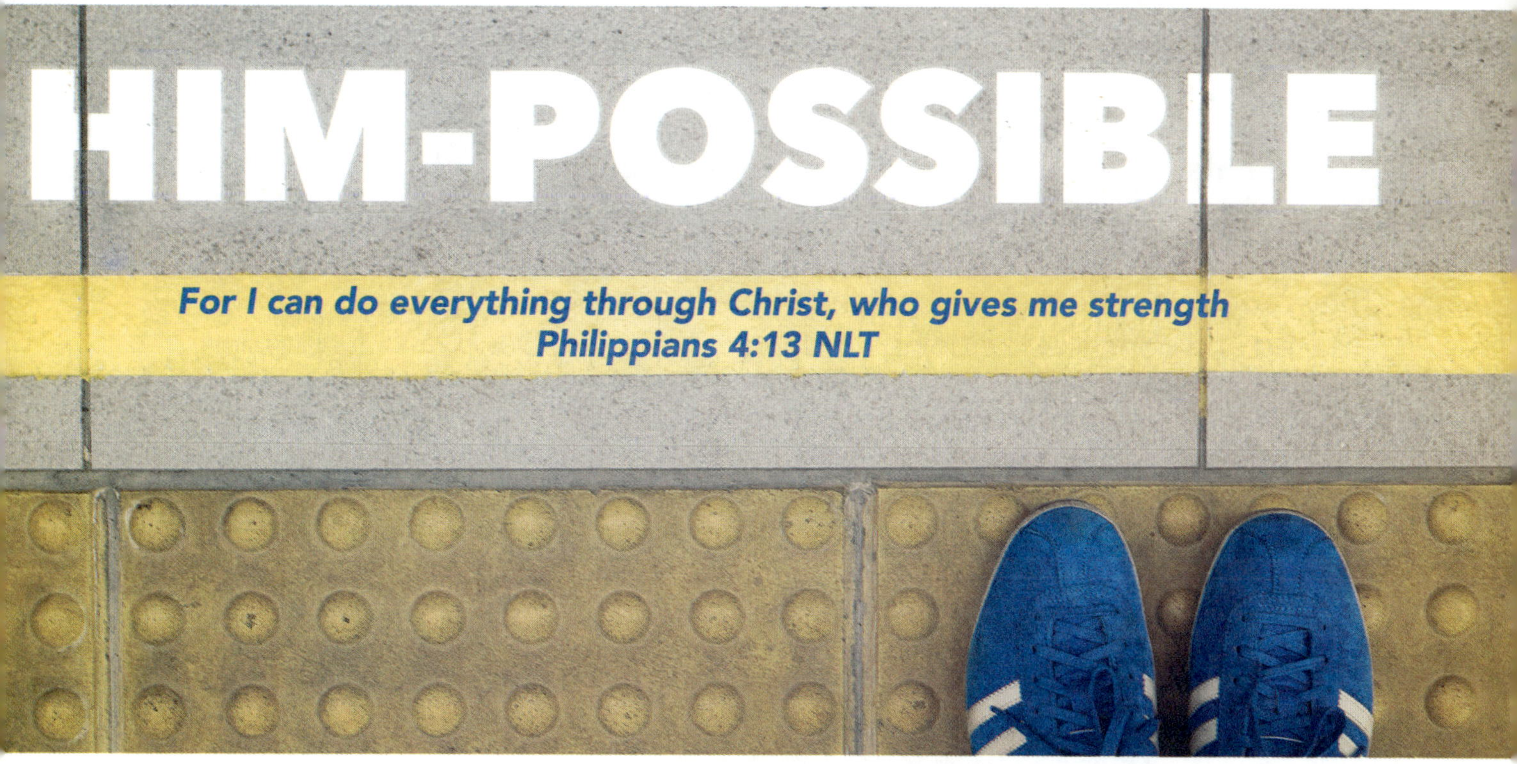
HIM-POSSIBLE
For I can do everything through Christ, who gives me strength
Philippians 4:13 NLT

Generate a Positive Attitude

...forgetting what lies behind and reaching forward to what lies ahead, I press on toward the goal for the prize of the upward call of God in Christ Jesus.   Philippians 3:13-14 NASB

Read, pray and exercise these verses to turn negative emotions - anger, fear and depression - into positive motivation and movement forward.

1. When anger holds you back, forget what lies behind by forgiving others for past hurts and loss, so you can emotionally move forward in freedom.
2. When fear pushes you back, reach forward to what lies ahead by overcoming with God's power, love and a sound mind.
3. When depression drags you down, build yourself up with strength training physically, mentally and spiritually.

Forget What Lies Behind

Overcome anger about the past. Have you been used, abused and refused? Have you lost your job, or are you in a job you wish you could lose? Are you making statements and experiencing feelings like these?

Work through the grieving process so God can heal you. Admit to yourself that whatever happened to you is true. Realize your feelings are legitimate. <u>Remember that what you do next matters most.</u>

Statements
This can't be. I don't believe it!
What do I do? How do I handle this?
They can't do that to me! I will get them!
I'm tired and don't feel like doing anything.
I don't feel well, headache, stomachache!

Feelings
Denial < - > Shock
Distraction < - > Panic
Irritation < - > Anger
Feeling Down < - > Depression
Stress < - > Physical Illness

*Be angry, and yet do not sin; do not let the sun go down on your anger, and do not give the devil an opportunity.
Ephesians 4:26-27 NASB*

Anger is One Letter Short of Danger

When you see red, danger lies ahead. Use these three steps to learn from and let go of the past.

1. Describe offenses and how you feel. List everyone you blame - others, you maybe God.

Describe the offense	How do you feel?	Offender's First Name

2. Forgive everyone you blame including yourself and/or God. Remember forgiveness is not a one-and-done event, but rather an ongoing exercise. Practice forgiveness anytime you feel irritation, frustration, anger, bitterness, wrath or rage. Don't wait until you feel like it. Take a deep breath and maybe a long walk. Make decisions to forgive for your own freedom and future.

3. Ask God to help you forgive by praying these verses…Trust & Obey There is no other way! If you hear Him, follow Him. **As read in** *John 14:21 NIV, "Whoever has my commands and keeps them is the one who loves me. The one who loves me will be loved by my Father, and I too will love them and show myself to them."*

"Dear Heavenly Father, I thank You for the riches of Your kindness, forbearance and patience, knowing that Your kindness has led me to repentance.

I confess that I have not extended that same patience and kindness toward others who have offended me, but instead I have harbored bitterness and resentment. I pray that during this time of self-examination, You would bring to mind only those people that I have not forgiven in order that I may do so. I ask this in the precious name of Jesus. Amen."

From *The Bondage Breaker* by Neil T. Anderson

Reach Forward to What Lies Ahead

Overcome fear in its various forms – nervousness, anxiety, fright, panic and terror. Reach forward to accept the opportunities that await you.

In Depth

Today is the first day of the rest of your life. You can make decisions now for the better that last forever. As you step into an unknown future, do not focus on the fear of making a mistake or failing, but rather ask yourself…

- How do I want to view my future?
- For what purpose am I here?
- How does God see me and my life?

Go back to pages 11-12 and read through Your Hope & Future exercise again. Write new or additional thoughts about your purpose and goals.

In Breadth

The good news is that America is the land of opportunity with millions of employers in more than 100 major industries employing over 150 million people in 1,000 major occupations. The bad news is that so many choices can make you anxious. Career exploration and job search requires so many activities - resumes, networking, interviews - that you can be overwhelmed. The fear of making a mistake can make you freeze.

Trust God and face the fear. Read and remember the truth in this verse…

What, then, shall we say in response to these things? If God is for us, who can be against us? …No, in all these things we are more than conquerors through him who loved us.

Romans 8:31 & 37 NIV

Face the Fear

Take courage! Fight the good fight with these one-two punches of truth.

For God has not given us a spirit of fear and timidity, but of power, love and self-discipline. 2 Timothy 1:7 NLT

There is no fear in love. But perfect love drives out fear, because fear has to do with punishment. The one who fears is not made perfect in love. 1 John 4:18 NIV

Now take these three steps to fight your fears…

1. List what makes you anxious, followed by actions to face fears based on the verses above…

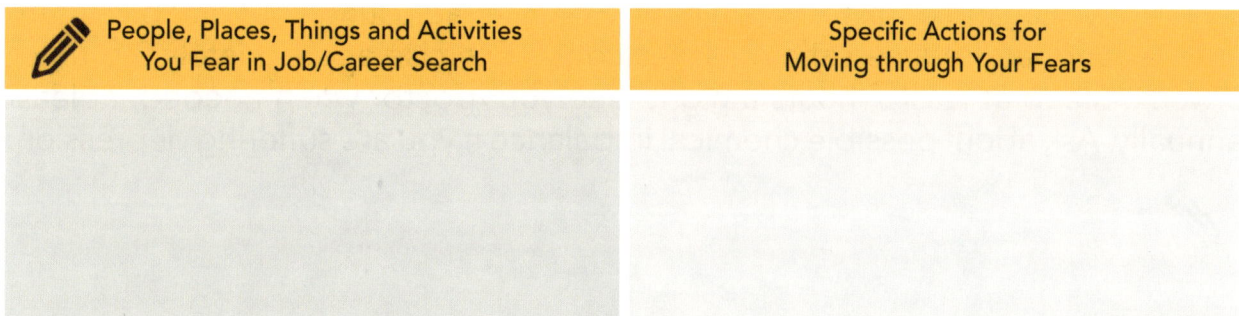

People, Places, Things and Activities You Fear in Job/Career Search	Specific Actions for Moving through Your Fears

2. Ask people who care about you whom you trust - family, friends, workmates, pastor - to pray for and encourage you.

Write Their Names Here

When fear appears, greet it with this prayer from Neil T. Anderson's *Freedom from Fear*:

"In the name and by the authority of the Lord Jesus Christ, I bind all lying spirits causing fear and anxiety in me. God has not given me a spirit of fear and timidity, but of power, love and discipline. I, therefore, reject all fear and choose to walk by faith in the Holy Spirit's power, live in the light of God's love, and think with the sound mind of Christ."

Press on Toward the Goal

*...but those who hope in the LORD will renew their strength.
They will soar on wings like eagles; they will run and not grow weary,
they will walk and not be faint. Isaiah 40:31 NIV*

Overcome depression with personal strength training, which generates much-needed energy and endurance for the journey ahead. To help you press towards the goal:

| Eat Right | + | Exercise | + | Get Lots Of Rest |

Read each section below and in the box that follows, write at least one goal for the section you just read.

Physically: Eat and drink the good stuff. Consider adjusting your diet by cutting calories and fat. Reduce caffeine and alcohol. Exercise appropriately 3-5 times a week. Sleep at least 7 hours a night. See your doctor when needed, at least annually. Ask about possible chemical imbalance if you are suffering depression.

Mentally: Feed your mind good thoughts. Spend time with good friends. Do things you enjoy. Get time alone when needed. Learn new things. See a professional counselor as needed.

Spiritually: Read <u>Go with God</u> again on pages 15-16. Pray for others and post requests on our confidential Prayer Network online. Read and study the Bible. Be active in a church.

Get More Help

Financial Stress can make a difficult job situation really tough. Three ways to alleviate financial pressure are to earn more, spend less or sell some stuff. Since you have more control over spending than earning, seek opportunities to cut spending and reduce your financial obligations. If you do not have a spending plan, make one. If you have debt, add it up and pay it down. If you own things you do not use, sell or give it away. The less money you need, the more freedom you have to accept the right job for you. Go to *crossroadscareer.org/money* for resources.

Family Issues might get worse in the midst of a career crossroads, but they can also improve. Tough times can stimulate husbands and wives to love, respect and support one another even better. Communication, collaboration and commitment are critical components.

Personal Problems can be better solved with help from others. Ask people who…

- You trust
- Care about you
- Possess the competency to help
- Have no vested interest in whatever you decide

Perhaps you might ask your best friend or good buddy; a church pastor or care minister; or a professional counselor.

1-800-DEAR-GOD
HEAVENLY BLUE PAGES

When in sorrow .... call John 14
When you have sinned ....call Psalm 51
When you worry .... call Matthew 6:19-34
When you are in danger..call Psalm 91
When God seems far away ....call Psalm 139
When your faith needs stirring .... call Hebrew 5:11
When you are lonely and fearful ....call Psalm 23
When you grow bitter and critical ....call 1 Corinthians 13
When you feel down and out .... call Romans 8:31
When you want peace and rest .... call Matthew 11:25-30
When the world seems bigger than God ....call Psalm 90
When you want Christian assurance.................................... call Romans 8:1-30
When you leave home for work or travel ....call Psalm 121
When your prayers grow narrow or selfish ....call Psalm 67
When you want courage for a task...call Joshua 1
When you think of investments and returns...................................call Mark 10
If you are depressed ....call Psalm 27
If your pocketbook is empty..call Psalm 37
If you are losing confidence in people............................. call 1 Corinthians 13
If people seem unkind .... call John 15
If discouraged about your work ....call Psalm 126
If pride takes hold ....call Psalm 19
If you want to be fruitful .... call John 15
For understanding of Christianity............................. call 2 Corinthians 5:15-19
For a great invention/opportunity..call Isaiah 55
For how to get along with fellow men .... call Romans 12
For Paul's secret to happiness ....call Colossians 3:12-17

Post prayers and praises on our confidential Prayer Network
crossroadscareer.org/prayer

33 Step Two Attitude

KEY TAKEAWAYS

What did you learn that was most important to you in this step?

Got questions or need help? Explore more Step 2 Resources online
crossroadscareer.org/step-2

STEP THREE
APTITUDE

For You God created my inmost being; You knit me together in my mother's womb. I praise You because I am fearfully and wonderfully made

Psalm 139:13-14 NIV

INWARD

Discover Your Best

There is no one like you anywhere. Never has been. Never will be. You are uniquely designed by God. No other person on the planet has your DNA and personal history.

Step Three Aptitude

5 Factors in Your Unique Design

The better you understand you, the better you can see how to maximize your career. Most professionals in career planning and development consider 5 factors.

Your Gifts
1. **Experiences** – Your history – personal, educational, vocational
2. **Abilities** – What you do best – talents, knowledge, skills
3. **Personality** – How you do best what you do – natural behavioral traits

Your Passions
4. **Interests** – What you like most – people, places, things, activities
5. **Values** – What is important to you – life purpose and principles

Love What You Do
Employ your passions, as well as your gifts. Research from *If It Ain't Broke, Break It* by Robert J. Kriegel and Louis Patler, proves the point:

"A team of researchers followed a group of 1,500 people over a period of 20 years. At the outset of the study, the participants were divided into 2 groups:

- Group A, 83% of the sample, was composed of people embarking on a career path they had chosen solely for the prospect of making money now in order to do what they wanted later in life.
- Group B, the other 17% of the sample, consisted of people who had chosen their career paths so that they could do what they wanted now and worry about the money later.

The data showed some startling revelations:

- At the end of the 20-year period, 101 of the 1,500 had become millionaires.
- Of the millionaires, 100 of the 101 were from Group B, the group that had chosen to pursue what they loved.

The key ingredient in most successful projects is loving what you do. Having a goal or a plan is not enough. Academic preparation is not enough. Prior experience is not enough. Enjoyment of your life's work is the key."

Introducing the X-Factor

The active presence of Jesus Christ in your life introduces the X factor into your unique design.

> *Therefore, if anyone is in Christ, he is a new creature;*
> *the old things passed away; behold, new things have come.*
> *2 Corinthians 5:17 NASB*

It begins the millisecond you are created anew in Jesus when you accept Him as your Savior and Lord. The Holy Spirit ignites the first 5 factors to manifest as spiritual gifts and God's calling.

What do you think about the X-Factor? Is it true? If you believe it is true, what will you do?

Write Your Thoughts...

How to Discover Gifts, Passions & Callings

- [ ] Complete self-assessments on pages 39-41
- [ ] Ask for Others' Input. See page 42
- [ ] Consider professional assessments and help on page 43
- [ ] Summarize what you learned on page 44

Inventory Your Experiences

List places you worked and the work you did from high school to the present. Make sure to include not only work for which you were paid, but also hobbies, volunteering, community projects, internships and extracurricular activities.

✎ **Work You Did** Occupations: jobs, titles, positions Examples: teacher, sales manager, clerk	**Places You Worked** Industries: employers and customers Examples: grocery store, school, military

You Are a STAR

Based on your experiences, describe the accomplishments you like best using the four-question STAR process.

1. What **Situation** did you face?
2. What **Tasks** were to be accomplished?
3. What **Actions** did you take?
4. What **Results** were achieved?

(handwritten: add beyond past work experience / focus on results / excitation / situations attacked)

Read this example.

Title: Increased sales performance in a newly assigned territory			
Situation you faced	**Tasks to accomplish**	**Actions you took**	**Results achieved**
Assigned new territory where sales declined 18% the prior year	Increase sales by 10% by the end of year	Surveyed customers. Identified a new competitor with a cheaper product. Put on a seminar for past, current and prospective customers featuring service	Regained 63% of past customers, added 27 new customers, and increased sales by 24%

Write a sample accomplishment using keywords, phrases and facts in the form below.

Title:			
Situation you faced	**Tasks to accomplish**	**Actions you took**	**Results achieved**

Write more STAR stories. Go to **crossroadscareer.org/star**

You Are an A+VIP

Help yourself and others see you as God's masterpiece. You can get an A+ as a Very Important Person. Review pages 39-40. List keywords, phrases and facts in the form below...

A — Abilities
What you do best: talents, knowledge, skills

V — Values
What is important to you: purpose, principles, burdens

I — Interests
What you like most: people, places, things, activities

P — Personality
How you do best what you do: natural behavioral traits

Step Three Aptitude

Ask For Others Input

List people who know you well from work, school, neighborhood, church or community in the space below...

 **Write Their Names Here**

Contact the names on your list. Consider using the following introduction, *"I am considering my career future and I would like your help. Would you have time to answer a few questions?"* See recommended questions below, which you can download from **crossroadscareer.org/resources**.

What do you see as my biggest accomplishments?

What do I do best? What do you see as my abilities, talents, knowledge, skills?

What words come to mind when describing my personality?

What do I seem to like best – people, places, things and activities?

What do I value – life purpose, issues I think important?

How would you describe my spiritual gifts and calling?

What are my blind spots – what can I improve?

Are there jobs and careers you think would be a good fit for me?

Step Three Aptitude

Handwritten notes at top:
www.myskillsmyfuture.org
www.careeronestop.org / ExploreCoachs
strenghfinders

Free Assessments & Help

Register/login at crossroadscareer.org

The Interest Profiler makes it quick and easy to rate what you like concerning people, places, things and activities, which helps you discover which occupational clusters are the best fit for you to explore.

- Realistic: practical, physical, concrete, hands-on, machine, tools
- Investigative: analytical, intellectual, scientific, explorative, thinker
- Artistic: creative, original, independent, chaotic, inventive, media, graphics
- Social: cooperative, supporting, helping, healing, nurturing, teaching
- Enterprising: competitive environments, leadership, persuading, status
- Conventional: detail-oriented, organizing, clerical

The Skill Matcher helps you identify careers that match your skills. You answer 40 questions to rate your level in a range of skills. Then you see a list of careers that are good matches for your unique set of skills. You can learn about average pay, typical education, and the outlook (new job opportunities expected) for jobs in that field.

Get Help

Taking assessments alone can be confusing. Consider getting free help from one of our partner ministry career coaches, counselors or consultants. Search crossroadscareer.org/locations.

If you want to explore hiring a career or job coach, counselor or consultant, consider these important factors:

- Review their experiences, qualifications and specialties
- Understand their services, features and benefits
- Ask about their fees and assessment costs
- Get the financial agreement in writing
- Expect a free initial consultation
- Talk to at least three references

Summarize Your Best

As each one has received a special gift, employ it in serving one another as good stewards of the manifold grace of God.
1 Peter 4:10 NASB

Explore all 6 factors to discover and develop your best to serve others.

1. **Experiences** – Your history – personal, educational, vocational
2. **Abilities** – What you do best – talents, knowledge, skills
3. **Personality** – How you do best what you do – natural behavioral traits
4. **Interests** – What you like most – people, places, things, activities
5. **Values** – What is important to you – life purpose and principles
6. **X-Factor** – What are your spiritual gifts. Hear God calling.

Review pages 41-45 along with all your assessments. Look for common themes, keywords and phrases, and write them in the form below.

	Gifts			Passions	
	Experiences, Your Background	Abilities, Talents, Skills, Knowledge	Personality, Behavior Traits	Interests, What You Enjoy	Values, What's Important

X-Factor – Spiritual Gifts and Calling

Step Three Aptitude

You Are God's Masterpiece

 For we are God's masterpiece. He has created us anew in Christ Jesus, so we can do the good things he planned for us long ago.

Ephesians 2:10 NLT

Do you think of yourself as a masterpiece? If not, consider the words of theologian Ken Boa:

"To love ourselves correctly is to see ourselves as God sees us and to allow the Word, not the world, to define who and whose we really are. The clearer we capture the vision of our new identity in Jesus Christ, the more we will realize that our deepest needs for security, significance and satisfaction are met in Him and not in people, possessions or positions."

Prayerfully ask God to show you what He sees in you. Write thoughts that come to your mind in the box below.

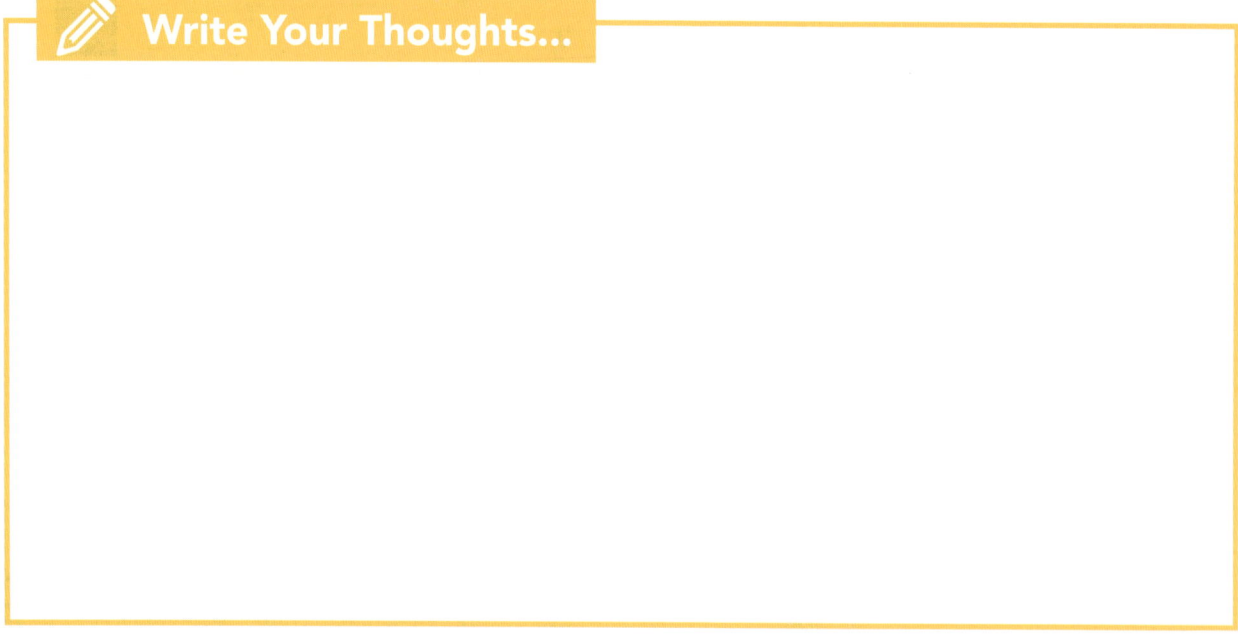

KEY TAKEAWAYS

What did you learn that was most important to you in this step?

_____

_____

_____

_____

_____

_____

_____

_____

Got questions or need help? Explore more Step 3 Resources online

crossroadscareer.org/step-3

INWARD

STEP FOUR
ALTITUDE

Each of you should use whatever gift you have received to serve others, as faithful stewards of God's grace in its various forms.

1 Peter 4:10 NIV

Target Opportunities

Attitude + Aptitude = Altitude. Get motivation and direction to target opportunities by doing what you do best for people who need it most.

How to Target Opportunities

Listed below are descriptions of targeting factors and how to explore each.

1. **Occupations** describe the work you do – the job functions you perform.
    You can easily and quickly search the database of almost 1,000 occupations in The Occupational Information Network (O*NET), America's primary source of occupational information.

   Visit *www.onetonline.org*. Select keywords and phrases from Summarize Your Best on page 44 and go exploring. Each occupation is described by worker abilities, interests, styles, values, skills, knowledge, education, experience, training, as well as job activities/tasks, position titles/descriptions, salaries/wages, and tools/technology with links to major associations and similar occupations.

onentonline.org

2. **Employers** are people and organizations for whom you work. Start by searching through more than 100 major industry groups of Industries at a Glance at www.bls.gov/iag. Each industry is described by types of organizations, occupations, earnings and employment trends.

3. **Locations** can be defined city, state, zip and even country. If you want to work where you live now, use your home zip code with occupational and employer keywords in our Job Connector search tool to not only see job postings but also to find places that are hiring. If you want to relocate and explore other locations, go to www.bestplaces.net.

4. **Income** is about salary, wages and benefits. To find out how much jobs pay, consider looking at websites like www.salary.com. Cash compensation is not only salary/wages, but also commissions, bonuses and tips. Benefits can include medical insurance and retirement/savings plans. For a helpful checklist, see pages 109-111, Understand Offers Better.

Be as flexible as possible on income needed by reducing your cost of living as much as you can, especially if you are changing careers, during which time you may have to earn less as you learn a new occupation or industry.

5. **Platforms** are about working as either an employee, self-employed contractor, business owner or volunteer.

You are an employee if the employer can control what work will be done and how it will be done. The employer withholds a portion of your income for taxes, Social Security and Medicare which are summarized annually on a W2 form. Some advantages include:

- Benefits like medical insurance, savings and retirement plans.
- Being part of an organization.
- Training and development.

You are a self-employed contractor if the employer only has the right to control the result of the work done, but not the means or methods. Employers do not withhold taxes on payments to contractors. Employers issue a 1099 statement to the contractor that summarize the earnings paid to a contractor, who is then responsible for paying taxes directly to the IRS. Advantages of being a contractor are:

Step Four Altitude

- Higher rates of pay for a job or project.
- Greater flexibility and freedom on how work gets done. Less supervision.
- Working for shorter periods of time. Having a wider variety of work.
- Contracting can lead to employment with the employer.

<u>Owning your own business</u> has higher risks and rewards. Be aware that half of startup businesses are out of business within 5 years. Apply the principles and practices in this workbook for best results. If you want more information about how to start or buy a business or franchise, contact the U.S. Small Business Administration at *www.sba.gov*.

<u>Volunteer</u> for two good reasons. First, you believe in what a particular organization is doing. Second, because volunteering provides experience and training, contacts and networking opportunities for a new career. It is a good way to see if you might like the work. Search volunteer openings at your church and in your community.

6. **Culture** <u>is about the operating values of an employer</u>.

Organizations have a way of getting things done revealing their values. Look for published value statements, usually found on the About page of their website. Most importantly, find and ask the following questions of current and past employees, customers and vendors:

- "What is it really like to work there?"
- "What do you like most and least?"
- "How would you describe their culture?"

Do the operating values of an employer match the keywords/phrases you used to describe your personal values on page 44? Hopefully yes! But, do not automatically reject an employer because of values mismatch. It is possible God will direct you to an employer that has different or even opposite values so you can be a light in a dark place. Know as much as you can about what you are getting into.

> Use all 6 targeting factors to analyze and describe what employers need most that you do best. Summarize with keywords, phrases, and facts in the Target Opportunities exercise on the next page.

Begin To Target Opportunities

Explore all 6 factors to help you target opportunities...

- Nearly 1,000 major occupations
- More than 100 major industries/employers
- Minimum and target income levels
- Your preferred locations
- Four different work platforms
- Best fit organizational cultures

Review How to Target Opportunities on pages 49-51. Use keywords, phrases and facts to complete this form.

Occupations	Employers

Locations	
Income	
Platforms	
Culture	

Not all targeting factors have the same importance to you. For example, the location may be most important because of family obligations. Occupation and Income might be more important to you than Industry.

Rank Most Important Factors 1 thru 6

Occupations _____   Employers _____   Locations _____

Income _____   Platforms _____   Culture _____

Step Four Altitude

Find Employers

Find employers who need most what you do best. Imagine you are a hand looking for a glove that fits. You fill employer needs by the handiwork you do. Start identifying target employers in preferred locations and industries through:

- Chambers of commerce
- Newspapers, business journal and magazine websites
- Professional and trade associations, clubs and user groups
- Online job postings

Once you identify a target employer, learn more by searching their websites about…

- Products, services and markets to learn what they do for whom.
- Organization mission, vision, values, size, scope and growth.
- Leader names and positions in areas you are interested in.
- Careers, opportunities and benefits.
- Job openings and descriptions.

If you do not see a job posting for you, it does not mean there are no openings. Most jobs that get filled are never listed anywhere.

Search for people who work for a target employer. Ask employees about their role, what they like and possible employment opportunities.

Learn more at **crossroadscareer.org/resources**

Attract Employers

Two very important messaging tools can attract employers to whether you are looking for a job or not:

1. Your profile on LinkedIn.com. For free you can post a career-focused profile which can be found by organizations seeking employees, consultants, vendors or partners.
2. Your resumes are more job search focused. Customize each targeted resume for a specific position and employer in which you are interested.

Develop both resumes and your profile using four key principles:

- Clearly communicate the target opportunities you seek
- Highlight what you do best that the employer needs most
- Feature STAR story results relevant to the employer
- Focus on the value you offer

Headline & Value Statements

Your profile and resume have about 7 seconds to attract attention to the value you offer. If employers like what they see, then they will read more. You must quickly communicate "what I can do for you."

Under your name at the top of your resume and profile, write a 3-10 word headline supported by three value statements. Think of it as a three-legged stool.

Write your headline explaining what you do that has value.

Then write value statements supporting your headline…

1. Employer needs that you seek to meet

2. What services, experiences, abilities and/or personal qualities you offer

3. The benefits that employers will receive from the work you do

Here are three examples of headlines and supporting value statements…

College CFO Achieves Savings & Growth

Seeking an educational organization that needs finance, accounting and process improvement. Offering 10 years experiences as a college CFO that achieved savings and growth.

Happy Administrative Help

Looking for a small business needing office management and customer service. Brings administrative abilities and an outgoing personality that improves efficiency and customer satisfaction.

Landscaper Increases Property Looks & Value

Searching for San Diego commercial real estate owners or managers that need landscaping. Provides skills, equipment and attention to detail that will keep the grounds looking great and the value high.

 Write A Headline With Value Statements About You

How to Write Your LinkedIn® Profile

Join for free or sign-in to _LinkedIn.com_, the world's largest professional network with more than 500 million users in more than 200 countries and territories worldwide, LinkedIn provides you a simple to use and powerful platform to develop your career and search for jobs. LinkedIn relies on matching of keywords to create relevancy between you and the searching party.

Your LinkedIn profile will consist of 6 core content sections and serve as the best place to use keywords.

1. A good <u>Headline</u> will attract people to help you get hired. The headline should not always reflect what you are currently doing, but what you would like to do next. You want your headline to entice viewers to read further.
2. <u>Summary</u> is a place for you to summarize your best in a scannable format keeping sentences short. Highlight results from assessments taken, skills and abilities possessed as well as inviting people to connect with you using your email address.
3. <u>Experience</u> highlights your work history. Be sure to provide 3-5 bullet points under each position you have held.
4. <u>Education</u> allows for you to list your schooling and training as well as brief descriptions and fields of study.
5. <u>Skills & Endorsements</u> highlights what you do best and provides opportunity for endorsements. Organize in order of most to least important.
6. <u>Interests</u> speaks more to who you are than what you do at work. Here you can connect with people of similar interests and values.

Then add two quality images:
1. A head and shoulders photograph of you that you like.
2. A background header image relevant to your occupation and/or industry.

Here are five more tips from LinkedIn on how to write your profile:

1. Focus on keywords: To improve your standing when employers search LinkedIn and Google, you'll want to include keywords that highlight your top skills.
2. Write how you speak. Think about how you would speak to someone you

met at a conference and write that way. Also, pack your LinkedIn profile with a personality that matches yours, but always keep it professional.

3. Show lots of white space: People have short attention spans, and many will skim your text. Steer clear of long, dense paragraphs. Use bullet points and sub-heads to make it easier on the eyes.
4. Add rich media: If you have a video, article or slide show about your work, share it.
5. Proofread: Your first draft should never be your final draft. Prepare to wrestle with words, move them around, and cut unnecessary ones. Ask other people for feedback. Make sure there are no grammar errors or typos.

Master Resume

Review your work-related files. Look for job performance reviews. Find whatever awards and rewards you have received. Search every thank you and "way-to-go" note and email. Review all your homework, assessments and counsel from pages 39-44.

Develop and continuously add to a <u>Master Resume</u> for your own use, from which you can find information for writing customized resumes for specific employers and jobs.

To develop a Master Resume, think of everything you have ever done, everything you want to promote, everything you did that is "above and beyond," including your STAR stories. You can download Master Resume forms from *crossroadscareer.org/master*.

Once you have written your headline and value statements, the next most important part of your resume content is to feature results.

Most employers, customers, recruiters and hiring managers believe that the best predictor of future success is past success. Put your most relevant STAR story achievements from page 40, in your resume, describing only the results in as few words as possible. Here is an example:

- Increased sales by 27% in the face of increased competition

Your goal is to catch the interest of readers, so they want to know how you got to the results you got.

Free Resume Command Center

Register/login at *crossroadscareer.org*, and then click on Resumes. You will see three ways to create and keep all your resumes in one place:

Resume Builder
Build your own from scratch with our easy to use builder.

Upload Resume
Upload your existing resume from Word or PDF.

Copy and Paste Resume
Choose this if you have an existing resume and would like to copy and paste it instead of uploading.

You can post or send your resumes directly to employers and recruiters on our Crossroads Career Job Connector that has thousands of job postings. You can also choose to be found by employers that are looking for candidates, or you can keep your resumes hidden if you are searching for jobs confidentially.

Resume Tips

Resume content, styles and formats are as varied as the people they represent. However, these three principles always apply.

- Resumes that get results show results.
- People do not read resumes. They quickly scan resumes.
- Don't write sentences. Use keywords, phrases, facts.

In General
- Resumes are usually one to two pages using 12-point type.
- Put best value and accomplishments on the top half of the first page.
- Never put anything on your resume that is not completely true.
- Put white space between resume sections and in margins.
- Use correct spelling and punctuation. Avoid "I" or "we".
- Ask others to review your resume re-read before you send.

Contact Information
- Keep it simple. Use the name by which you usually introduce yourself.
- Add your email and mobile phone number. You may add your metro area or city and state if relevant.
- To protect your privacy, do not share postal or street address.
- Add your website if you have one, as well as your LinkedIn profile address.

Profile
- Begin with your Headline and Value Statements.
- Then add your most recent accomplishments that are relevant to the employer you are approaching.
- If you are continuing in your same career, consider placing your STAR story situations and results in the Experience section of your resume.
- If you are changing, entering or re-entering your career, you can cluster your STAR story situations and results from the strengths that you want to emphasize.
- You can borrow content from your LinkedIn profile, but unlike your LinkedIn profile, do not use words like "I, my or your."
- You can also add new results, keywords, phrases or facts in order to further customize your resume for a particular job.

Experience
- List employment in reverse historical order – most recent job or employer first.
- Give basic employer or self-employed information such as organization name, city, state, dates. You can add a phrase that describes what the organization does.
- List job function or position titles with dates, responsibilities and activities.
- If you are continuing your current career direction, briefly describe STAR story situations and results beside the related jobs.
- If you are changing, entering or re-entering your career, briefly mention results only beside related jobs.
- Include military, missionary and ministry work experience if relevant.

Education
- Show each school, degree, major and academic accomplishment.
- Omit high school if you have a college degree of more than 10 years ago.
- List significant extracurricular activities and employment while attending school.
- Add additional training, development and certifications as is relevant.
- Add language and technical skills including computer proficiencies.

Interests
- List selected work, employer or relationship interests
- Organizations to which you belong
- Community activities and awards
- Hobbies, activities and travel

Do Not Include (unless relevant to job or employer)
- Compensation information
- Personal interests or activities
- Gimmicks, colors, fancy borders, shading, graphics, photographs
- Reasons for leaving previous positions
- References available upon request or names of references

Little White Lies Are Big Black Holes

A false witness will not go unpunished, and whoever pours out lies will not go free. Proverbs 19:5 NIV

Almost without thinking, you utter a tiny little lie. Then, when the truth confronts it, you tell another lie to protect the first lie. Then the truth comes again, so you lie again.

What began as a little white lie becomes a pack of lies consuming truth that is sucked into a big black hole. Instead, remember that the truth works better than anything else.

Recheck your resumes and profile. Any lies hiding anywhere in there?

*This page is intentionally left blank, feel free to use this area for notes.

KEY TAKEAWAYS

What did you learn that was most important to you in this step?

_____
_____
_____
_____
_____
_____
_____
_____
_____

Got questions or need help? Explore more Step 4 Resources online

crossroadscareer.org/step-4

*This page is intentionally left blank, feel free to use this area for notes.

OUTWARD

LOVE
OTHERS
COMPASSIONATELY

GET THE RIGHT JOB

STEP FIVE
SEARCHING

The steps of a man are established by the Lord, and He delights in his way.

Psalm 37:23 NASB

OUTWARD

Seek to Serve

Rather than just search for a job or career, seek to serve others. Everything changes when you serve as a faithful steward of God's grace. First of all, God is pleased. Secondly, people are more attracted to you.

Giving Versus Getting

With your focus on giving versus getting, you will attract others into your search. It is through serving that relationships are built, which leads to communities of help and hope. When you are seeking to serve, be sure to use both eyes…

One eye is for looking according to your plans. 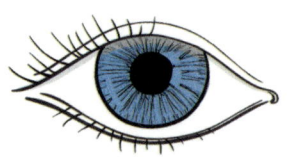 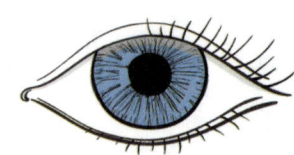 **The other eye is for seeing as God directs.**

Finding the right opportunity comes from seeing something you are not seeking that is even better than you planned because God prepared it for you.

The mind of man plans his way, but the Lord directs his steps.
Proverbs 16:9 NASB

Spiritually Strategic

Searching for jobs may be a challenge for you if you are not sure where to start, not experienced networking with people you do not know, and/or not comfortable using the internet. Instead, learn to seek to serve others by using this three-part strategy:

| Pray Continually | + | Connect Personally | + | Search Virtually |

Pray Continually

Ask and it will be given to you; seek and you will find;
knock and the door will be opened to you.
Matthew 7:7 NIV

Imagine you are dialing 1-800-Dear-God. Call the One Person who knows everything, everyone, everywhere, all the time. Ask His help every day before every meeting, phone call, text and email. Get linked in and stay connected with the Lord! See page 33.

Connect Personally

Building relationships and getting personal referrals are the most effective ways to find and get jobs. Consider this verse as you seek to serve others.

Do nothing out of selfish ambition or vain conceit. Rather, in humility value others above yourselves, not looking to your own interests but each of you to the interests of the others
Philippians 2:3-4 NIV

Here are two reasons to connect personally with others:

1. **50-85% of jobs that get filled are never posted anywhere**. Before advertising job openings, most employers network for candidates through personal referrals. You can only find opportunities in this huge hidden job market by connecting with others.

2. **Personally referred candidates are 42 times more likely to be hired**, according to a private corporate study. Referred candidates are more likely to be favorably received because of the positive reputation of the person making the referral, as well as the higher likelihood of matching personal values with corporate culture.

Prepare to connect and build community…

- Seek to serve everyone you meet.
- Be clear about who needs most what you do best.
- Know the jobs for which you want to interview.
- Research employers for which you want to work.
- Write a bullet-point script of what you are going to say.
- Identify hiring managers by position title and ideally by name.

Prepare before you reach out. Learn something about each contact before connecting. Write out points you want to make. Start your communication with the name of whoever referred you. Know what you need to know. Always be prayerful, intentional and alert.

Start Connecting Now

Pray and make a list of people you know: family, friends, neighbors, work associates, past acquaintances, former schoolmates, etc. Start with a few names on the lines below.

Contact	Company	Phone/Email	Referral

Use a contact management system or a networking log to track contacts. Record who referred whom in what organizations, so you can follow-up. Network and stay organized every day. Review and preview progress every week using page 19.

> **Act wisely toward outsiders, making the most of the time. Let your speech always be gracious, seasoned with salt, so that you may know how you should answer each person.**
>
> **Colossians 4:5-6 CSB**

Connect 4 Ways

1. **Online networks and social media**, such as LinkedIn, Facebook, Twitter and Instagram, provide effective ways to connect, with the added advantage of discovering information about each person. See pages 79-80.

2. **Email, texts and letters** can be efficient, but may not be personal. They are best for quick introductions, confirmations and follow-ups. It also is a great way to share your resume, bio or Linkedin profile.

3. **Phone calls** are both efficient and effective. You can have as many as five personal and productive conversations per hour. Follow-up with a brief email and maybe even a personal meeting.

4. **In-person** meetings can be the most effective – either by face-to-face or video conference. In-person meetings also happen in group settings such as job fairs, networking events, study classes, career centers, association or community meetings.

Emails & Letters

Put your best thoughts in writing and send them directly to the person you want to reach.

The great thing about writing is that it forces you to be clear about what you want and how you can help. The advantage of email is speed and ease of sending, receiving, replying and forwarding. The advantage of postal mail is that few people actually use it anymore, which means you will absolutely stand out.

Emails and letters are most useful for three purposes:

1. An introduction that includes your resume.
2. A follow-up request for information or contacts.
3. A thank you after networking or interviewing.

Get your own email address. Do not use your work email for personal reasons, especially for job search. "At least two-thirds of employers monitor workers' email, and half have fired employees as a result. What's more, they're in their rights to do so," The ePolicy Institute. Go to crossroadscareer.org/step-5 and read the "Get Your Own Email" article.

Step Five Searching   70

To maximize the effectiveness of your personal email, create an address that features your name, such as john.smith@gmail.com or jsmith@yahoo.com. Do not use cute or inappropriate email addresses, such as hotmama@me.com or silverfox@aol.com. Avoid nonsensical numbers, names or codes, like 321xyz@inbox.com.

More tips to make your email more effective include:

- Consider using proofreading tools like Grammarly.com to check for errors.
- Put your email address in resumes, business cards, letters – everything!
- Put at the bottom of your emails your name, phone and email.
- Confirm appointments the day before your meeting or interview.
- After every phone conversation, email a thank you.
- Write short emails. Fewer words equal more communication.
- When being referred, put the referring person's name in the subject line.
- When emailing a resume, save your resume using your name and specialty.

Emails and letters will help you to set up phone calls and in-person meetings.

 **Connect by Phone**

Prepare before making calls to decrease anxiety and increase effectiveness.

- Pray to connect with the One Who knows everyone. Thank, praise and ask God for help before and after every call.
- Find a quiet place with no distractions, such as a closed room in your home, or even in your parked car facing away from traffic or activity.
- Write down the name of the person you are calling, their organization, phone number and bullet-point script. Keep your networking script handy.
- Wear earbuds or headphones to maximize the quality of the call. Avoid using the speaker or Bluetooth. Use a laptop, tablet or pen/paper to write keyword notes.
- Text messages can be effective with people you know for forwarding files and links, as well as asking if they are available for a call.

While you are calling, you will face challenges. Some additional tips include:

- If you call and get voicemail, then leave a message starting with your name and the name of the person who referred you along with your phone number.
- If someone else answers, tell them your name and who referred you. Ask if the person you are calling is available. If not, you can leave a voicemail.
- Practicing calls with people you know helps you get comfortable with what you want to say, and it confirms that your phone connection is as clear as possible.
- Take a few minutes between calls to walk around, stretch, go to a restroom, drink some water – so you can refresh yourself and be ready for the next call.

 **Sample Phone Conversation**

Let's pretend you are calling Mary Jones, who was referred by Bill Smith. You are considering a career transition into an accounting position in a bank where Mary works. You dial the phone, it rings, and someone answers: *"Hello..."*

Be attentive to what you hear. Does the person answering sound angry, happy, confused, depressed? Is there background noise or people talking?

You begin by saying *"Hi, this is (your first and last name), and I was referred by Bill Smith. Is this Mary Jones?"* Mary answers, *"Yes."*

You begin by saing, *"Is now a good time to talk, or would another time be better?"* Do not press for now, especially if you hear Mary sounding down, distracted or there is background noise. If she says later is better, then ask, *"When are the best days and times for you?"* Mary asks, *"What do you want to talk about?"*

You answer, *"Bill suggested you would be a great person to talk to. I am exploring new career opportunities and want to ask for your advice and counsel. Maybe a phone call – no more than 15 minutes – at your convenience?"*

Step Five Searching 72

Mary replies, "Oh, glad to help! Actually, now would be better than later. What do you want to know?"

You ask for the information you want. Maybe you want suggestions of banks that fit certain criteria, advice on how to approach hiring managers, or connections within accounting departments.

You also might say, "I am networking for referrals to bank accounting directors. Who do you know in the top five banks here? I am seeking to serve..." Read from your elevator pitch the 3 parts of your value statements. Be ready if Mary starts asking questions about your experience and interests. Keep a copy of your resume and STAR stories close by.

Check your watch. As you see the 15-minute mark coming, begin to wrap up your call.

"I want to be thoughtful of your time. Would you like a copy of my resume in case you think of someone or something later? What is your email address?" Repeat Mary's email address to confirm you got it right.

Conclude your call with appreciation. Consider a combination of these types of wrapping-it-up statements...

- "Thank you for your time."
- "You have been very helpful."
- "If I have an additional question, may I call you back?"
- "If there is anything I can do for you, please let me know."
- "Have a great day!"

After the Call

- Thank God for the call. Ask Him for favor through the connection.
- Write down notes and next steps about the conversation.
- Send a follow-up email with a copy of your resume.
- Call, text or email a "thank you" to the referring person.
- Continue to improve your scripts as needed.

 ## Get Up Close & In-Person

Take the time and make the effort to meet and greet three groups of people who can help you connect personally…

1. **Job Support and Networking Groups**

   Many church, community, and professional groups have regular meetings that offer opportunities to connect. Be sure to take networking cards and resumes, as well as your networking list and notepad. Find groups on crossroadscareer.org/locations or search local newspaper sites.

2. **American Job Centers**

   More than 2,000 American Job Centers cover every county in the United States. Funded primarily by the U.S. and state departments of labor, these centers offer free job search and career exploration, educational funding, vocational training and unemployment assistance. To find a job center near you go to our resource section at careeronestop.org

3. **Career and Job Fairs**

   Look for local opportunities to meet employers and recruiters face-to-face, usually listed on newspaper and community websites. Some job fairs feature one employer with many openings. Other fairs include multiple employers focused on a particular community, occupation, industry or school.

How to intentionally prepare for a career or job fair

- ☐ Get and review the list of registered employers.
- ☐ Identify and research the employers you want to meet.
- ☐ Walk the floor to find out who is where.
- ☐ Greet each employer of interest with a smile and handshake, while you tell them your first and last name.
- ☐ Ask for a few minutes to talk about jobs of interest to you.
- ☐ Be ready to give them your networking card and tell them what you do best that matches the job you want.
- ☐ Do not be surprised if you have an interview on the spot.
- ☐ Ask for their business card and any literature they may have.
- ☐ Ask for a follow-up meeting or phone call.

# Recruit Recruiters

The best method for finding good recruiters is to ask your friends, networking contacts and employers. Research recruiters and work with those you trust who seem to have your best interest at heart. Meet them in person if at all possible.

Basically, there are two kinds of recruiters:

<u>Recruiters who are employees of an employer</u> should be very knowledgeable about their organization, current job openings, and the hiring process. Their role is to find and qualify candidates, guide them through the hiring process, and advise the hiring manager on making the best hire.

<u>Recruiters who work for recruiting firms</u> usually specialize either by occupation or industry. While these recruiters may not know as many details about the employer or the jobs, they can be very effective in getting you introduced in a positive way. There are three types of recruiting firms…

- Staffing firms are paid by employers to recruit for part-time, temporary, and/or "permanent" non-management positions. Some staffing firms put you on their payroll and may provide benefits as you work for their client employers.

- Contingency recruiting firms are paid by an employer contingent upon the company hiring a person referred by the recruiter. They usually handle full-time positions that pay less than $100,000.

- Retained recruiting firms are paid in advance by employers to fill a specific executive, management, professional and board of director position. Positions they represent on an exclusive basis usually pay over $100,000 annual salary. <u>Beware</u> of recruiters who ask you to sign documents other than reference consent or background investigation forms. Do not sign written agreements that obligates you to pay any fee or gives any firm the exclusive right to represent you.

Networking Scripts & Cards

Imagine you are in an elevator. Someone gets on that you know, and they ask about how you are doing. You tell them you are searching for a new job/career/work, and they ask, "What are you looking for?" You have less than 30 seconds to respond. What do you say?

30 Second "Elevator Pitch"

Writing value statements for your resume and LinkedIn profile are important, but it is very different to verbalize them as part of a networking conversation. The words might be the same, but now you add voice quality and intonation, plus facial expressions and body language, all in the context of introducing yourself or answering a question.

Whether called an elevator pitch, personal commercial or a networking speech, you will help yourself by writing a networking script and practicing it. You can communicate what you are looking for and the value you offer by using a 3-part message:

1. What employers need the most.
2. What do you do best that meets those needs.
3. What value will employers receive from the work you do.

Go to the next page to practice writing networking scripts. You may think 30 seconds is not enough time, but you can actually speak 70-80 words without rushing. It is enough time to not only "make the pitch," but also greet someone, close by asking for "who do you know," and hand them a networking card.

Networking Card

Carrying resumes everywhere can be cumbersome. Not being able to give people a written description of your value statement, name and contact information is not acceptable. You can order 100 business cards for networking for $20 or less online or at an office supply or shipping store. Here is a super simple example…

Your Name
505-555-1234
Your.Name@Email.com

Accounting, Process Improvement, Leadership For Schools, Colleges and Universities looking to achieve substantial savings.

Step Five Searching

 # Write Your Networking Scripts

The most effective networking conversations focus on relationship building and seeking to serve. When it's your turn to share what you are seeking and the value you offer, use this 3-part message.

1. What employers need the most.
2. What do you do best that the employer needs most?
3. What value will employers receive from the work you do.

<u>Now Write Your Own Script</u>. Practice, practice, practice with friends, family, colleagues, anyone and everybody. Make improvements continuously.

Part 1: Describe the employer's needs that you seek to meet...

Part 2: List experiences, abilities, personality, interests and values that meet the needs...

Part 3: Describe the value that employers will receive from the work you do...

Online Searching

If you are looking for a job, spend 15% to no more than 50% of your search time online. Don't apply to everything you see. Carefully select positions that match your target opportunities. We recommend you use a combination of…

- Crossroads Career Job Connector
- LinkedIn and Social Media
- Employer Websites

 **Job Connector**

Register/Login at crossroadscareer.org to search our Job Connector for thousands of employer-posted jobs, plus you can:

- Set up email job alerts.
- Apply for jobs and track applications.
- Create, keep, post and send resumes and cover letters.
- Use the Interest Profiler and Skill Matcher assessments.
- Access our 7-step action plan, career and job resources.
- Post, pray, and praise on our confidential Prayer Network.

We also provide you with access to other online Super Job Sites…

- #1 world's largest job site with thousands of postings
- Christian jobs with churches and ministries
- Federal government and military jobs and careers
- Local newspapers and publications
- Freelance, part-time, temporary and hourly employment

Consider these tips for searching online job postings:

- If you are unemployed, search every day.
- If you are employed, search every weekend.
- Experiment with keywords, phrases and locations.
- Use automatic search agents for alerts about new job postings.
- When you apply for jobs include keywords in the posting that are true of you.

Posting your resume online? Only if your job search is not confidential. If you are employed and concerned that your employer may find you searching, then do not post your resume on any site. If your search is not confidential, post your resume selectively on the most relevant niche-market or employer sites. Other tips include…

- Edit your online resumes at least monthly to keep them "active and current."
- Monitor how many hits your resume gets. If too few or none, try new keywords.
- Do not pay extra to "boost" your resume's visibility.
- Never give your social security or other confidential numbers to anyone.
- Do not give any information or fill out any forms until you verify site credibility.

If you are interested in exploring your own business, you can find help and connections.

- The U.S. Small Business Administration offers programs, services and tools
- Explore the International Franchise Association for more opportunities

How to Grow Your LinkedIn® Network

As the world's largest professional network, LinkedIn provides a powerful platform to network for personal referrals, common interests, job postings and organizations.

If you have not yet built your free LinkedIn profile, go to pages 56-57. If you have a LinkedIn profile, check to be sure it is up-to-date. Next, sign into LinkedIn and look for people you know.

- Enter their name in the search bar.
- Look through alumni page of schools you attended.
- Search companies where you work currently or have worked.
- Check the "People You May Know" section.
- Import your email contacts.

Send personal invitations to connect with people who have the following in their personal profile: 50+ connections, photo, experience and education. Include a personal note related to something you have in common. For those who accept your invitation, look through their profile for common experiences, interests, organizations and people you may know. Send them a thank-you message for connecting. Ask if you can help them with their career and ask who they may know in your target occupations, industries or employers.

 **Social Media**

Social websites like Facebook, Twitter, Instagram, Snapchat, Pinterest and YouTube can be helpful for networking.

Warning! If you are already registered on one or more sites, be aware that 92% of all recruiters check your social media, so <u>be very careful not to show...</u>

- Drug or alcohol use.
- Spelling or grammar errors.
- Too much skin or too many selfies.
- Profanity, negative talk, political rants.

Do show a positive professional presence, as well as family, friends, personal interests and hobbies. Invite your social media contacts to connect with you on LinkedIn.

 **Employer Websites**

The most direct way to learn about target opportunities is through employer websites. Start with employers you listed as target opportunities on workbook page 52. Search at least once a week for new information about their products, services, management and (of course) job postings. Pay particular attention to names and positions of people with whom you want to connect.

Job applications: Before applying for a job or posting your resume on an employer website, do everything you can to get personal referrals to connect with employees, especially relevant hiring managers, recruiters and human resources representatives.

If you have the opportunity to either apply for a position and/or post a customized-just-for-them resume, do it carefully. For larger employers that use applicant tracking systems, be prepared with these tips...

- If applying for a specific job, be sure you are qualified.
- Review the application to be sure you have all the information ready.
- Answer all questions, including current, history or desired salary if asked.
- Do not exaggerate or misrepresent any information.
- Do not list references without their permission.

*This page is intentionally left blank, feel free to use this area for notes.

KEY TAKEAWAYS

What did you learn that was most important to you in this step?

Got questions or need help? Explore more Step 5 Resources online
crossroadscareer.org/step-5

OUTWARD

STEP SIX
SORTING

Do not use harmful words, but only helpful words, the kind that build up and provide what is needed, so that what you say will do good to those who hear you.

Ephesians 4:29 GNT

How To Wow Interviewers

Are you confident that your next interview will result in a job offer? For most of us, the answer is probably "No." But how great would it be to hear an interviewer say at the end of an interview, "Wow! That was impressive!"

Job-Winning Interviews

Let no unwholesome word proceed from your mouth, but only such a word as is good for edification, according to the need of the moment, so that it will give grace to those who hear.

Ephesians 4:29 NASB

All candidates must meet minimum qualifications to be selected, but the biggest difference in getting an offer is being prepared and passionate about the job, employer and the opportunity to interview. Increase your chances of hearing "yes" in your next interview whether by phone, in person or online.

- Connect what you do best with what employers need most.
- Be likable. People hire people they like. Get and keep a positive attitude.

Be Prepared & Passionate

First, do your homework on the employer and the job. Write down what you like about the opportunity. Make a list of concerns and questions.

Second, outline a one-page interview discussion guide that includes:

- Your name and contact information, employer's name, and the job to be done.
- Summary of positive facts about the employer.
- Your best attributes that summarize what you can do for the employer.
- Your career value and goals that match the opportunity the employer is offering.

Third, select STAR stories *(see page 40)* about your accomplishments that relate most to the employer's needs. Each story answers four questions.

- What was the Situation you faced?
- What was the Task to be accomplished?
- What were the Actions you took?
- What were the Results you got?

Fourth, if you do not feel confident and skilled in speaking, consider membership in a local Toastmasters club, where you can learn and practice how to tell your stories, listen and respond.

85   Step Six Sorting

Types of Interviews

Not only are there many types of interviews, there are also may ways that they may be conducted: by phone, in person, and online via live video conference or by texting in a chat room.

Qualifying or Screening Interviews

These interviews are usually 15 minutes to one hour by telephone. Try to be in a quiet place with no distractions. Have your resume and notes about the employer and position at hand. You might stand and smile in order to increase your energy and positivity.

If an interviewer calls without an appointment and you are not ready, ask for a few minutes to call back or schedule another time. If an interviewer calls representing an employer with which you have no contact or never heard of, beware of a possible scam.

Qualifying interviews usually focus on basic minimum candidate criteria, such as experience, education and specific skills. If asked about salary, try to delay until after you gain a better understanding of the job. You can ask questions, but some screening interviewers may not know much about the job.

Behavioral Interviews

Interviews that include behavioral questions are often an hour or more and can be conducted by phone, video conference or face-to-face. The interview focuses on specific situations and accomplishments. The questions often begin with phrases such as, "Can you tell me about a time when…?" or "Would you describe a situation that…?"

The interviewer is not only exploring your accomplishments, but also your personality traits, approach to problem-solving, communication abilities, your values in action, and how you handle challenging situations.

Respond with a STAR story that is most relevant to the question asked and the needs of the employer. Be specific, detailed and concise. Try to answer within 15- to 60-seconds, so that the question and answer might become a conversation.

Hiring Manager Interviews

This interviewer is usually the person to whom you will report if you are hired. The interview is usually in person lasting an hour or more, but sometimes it will be by video conference or phone. When you meet, ask about their background and current position. Seek to serve them by asking questions about what they want to be accomplished. Be alert for opportunities to connect relationally. Take notes for your follow-up email.

Sequential Interviews

It is not unusual to interview with a variety of people one after another – not only the hiring manager and human resources representative but also others involved in the hire.

Team or Panel Interviews

Two or more people might interview you at the same time. The advantage is that you have a chance to see how they interact.

Presentation Interviews

You may be asked to give a presentation followed by Q&A. This approach is common for sales positions. It gives you a chance to show your communication abilities.

Stress Interviews

Sometimes interviewers ask difficult questions in hard ways. No matter how frustrating or intimidating, do not fear or be angry. Pray for wisdom, strength and courage.

Introductory Interviews

You might be introduced to a senior executive for a 5 to 15-minute meeting. Take advantage of the opportunity to share your appreciation for the organization and job.

Engage Interviewers

Pray-Prepare-Perform-Praise

A good man brings good things out of the good stored up in his heart, and an evil man brings evil things out of the evil stored up in his heart. For the mouth speaks what the heart is full of.
Luke 6:45 NIV

 **Pray**

Fill your heart with good and positive thoughts from the Bible, such as praying verses from Psalms or your favorite devotionals.

Take your concerns and questions to God in prayer. Ask God to help you receive His vision, wisdom and strength.

Ask others to pray for you by posting a confidential prayer request in the Prayer Network on our website at **crossroadscareer.org/prayer.**

 **Prepare**

Especially encouraging before the interview is one of the most powerful and practical promises in the Bible from Philippians 4:6-7 NIV

Do not be anxious about anything, but in every situation, by prayer and petition, with thanksgiving, present your requests to God.

And the peace of God, which transcends all understanding, will guard your hearts and your minds in Christ Jesus.

Remember the verses above as you complete the preparations below…

Research the employer and job by visiting their website and searching online to read and print key information about who they are, what they do, recent news, careers and job description.

Make a file folder to take with you to the interview that shows you are prepared. Review homework suggested on workbook page 85. Put important information for your reference in the folder such as...

- Date, time and directions to interview location
- Information about the employer and interviewer
- A one-page interview discussion guide
- Selected STAR stories
- Relevant assessments and samples of your work
- Extra copies of your resume
- Writing pad and pen
- Put employer name on tab of folder

Do not give the folder to the interviewer, but share, as appropriate, items from the folder during the interview.

Practice interviewing with a friend or coach using questions on pages 93-96.

Rest and refresh. Eat right, exercise and get plenty of rest the day before.

Dress for success. Ask the employer about appropriate attire, which varies depending on the organization and the job to be done. If you need a haircut, get it. Trim wild hairs everywhere – ears, nose, neck and eyebrows. If you need new clothing, buy or borrow them. If your clothes need cleaning, do it. Read, write and review the Dress for Success devotional on page 101.

Never be late for an interview. Plan to arrive at least 15 minutes early. Leave yourself twice as much time as you think you will need to get ready and get to the interview.

Double-check directions the day before the interview. Fill up the car with gas. Know how much travel time it will take, where to park, how much it will cost. Lay out your interview clothes, clean shoes and folder the night before. Set your alarm.

Interview day final preparations. Do not push the snooze button. Pray and get going. Listen to music for inspiration – it's game time! Shower and shave. Floss and brush your teeth. Take breath mints. Comb or brush your hair. Do use deodorant. Apply lighter versus heavier makeup. Wear little or no jewelry. Do not wear cologne or perfume. Be sure you have everything you need. Check yourself in the mirror before you leave.

When you approach the interview location, be aware that you might be seen by the interviewer before the interview. Go to the restroom to make sure your hair is neat, your clothes are straight, your shoes are clean, and your confidence is in place with a smile on your face. Take a deep breath. Repeat in your mind "I can do all things through Christ who strengthens me" from Philippians 4:13.

 **Perform**

Present yourself at the main entrance, office or reception 15 minutes before the interview. If offered something to drink, politely decline. Be nice to everyone. Look around the waiting room. Browse displayed company literature. Stand while you wait, remembering that you are seeking to serve as God gives you the opportunity. Silently pray that the Holy Spirit will teach you what to say during the interview.

Greet the interviewer with a warm smile and a firm handshake. Look them in the eyes. Tell them how glad you are to meet them. If you are in their office, look for family photos, certificates or awards and ask questions or comment. Let the interviewer take the lead.

Most interviews have three parts, but not always in this order…

1. Interviewer describes the job. If you brought a copy of the job posting and/or description, ask if you may pull it from your folder and take notes. Seek to understand not only responsibilities, duties and activities, but also what needs to be accomplished.

    Ask about the organizational structure around the job. If you are interviewing with the direct report for the job, ask about their job and their background. If you are not interviewing with the direct report, ask the interviewer about the position and person to whom the position reports.

    Repeat important points to be sure you heard correctly. Ask about opportunities in which to contribute and grow. You can also ask what they are looking for in a successful candidate. State your appreciation for the information offered to you.

    If you are interested, say so and why. If you are not interested, say so and why the opportunity is not a fit for you.

2. Interviewer asks questions. Answer confidentially and honestly. Share relevant STAR stories. Limit answers from a few seconds to a couple of minutes.

    Feel free to pause to arrange your thoughts. If you do not understand a question, ask for clarification. Always be positive, and never say anything negative.

Step Six Sorting

3. <u>Present what you do best</u>. When the interviewer asks if you have more questions, respond by saying, "Instead of asking questions, may I have a few moments to share with you a brief discussion guide I prepared for our meeting?"

   When the interviewer says "yes," ask to move closer so you can point your way through the one-page interview guide on page 85. When you review contributions that you think you can make, say "I don't know everything about the position, but I would like to share how I think I can help. I would appreciate your feedback."

   Hopefully, good discussion follows. Close by saying "Because this position appears to match what I do best with what you need most, I would like the opportunity to work here and contribute." Wait for the interviewer to respond.

Usually, no commitment is given by the interviewer one way or another. Thank the interviewer. Say you enjoyed the interview and learning about the organization and job opportunity. Ask when you might hear about the next step. Take notes on what is said.

If you are interested in the opportunity, repeat why and how you can help. Mention what they appreciated about your candidacy. If there is another opportunity in the same organization that appears to be a better fit, ask about it. Whatever the situation and no matter how you feel, always send notes of appreciation. Send by email and postal mail on nice stationery.

If you are interested and do not hear back from the employer by the agreed upon date, make a follow-up call and/or send an email to underscore your interest. Consider following up once a week for seven weeks as persistence pays off. If you still hear nothing, then let it go, and continue to thank God for the experience.

Praise

Whether you feel the interview went well or not, praise God from Whom all blessings flow. God wastes nothing that happens to us. It may be an opportunity for a new career or a chance to learn how to interview better next time. Review what the employer said they appreciated about you, your experience, education, abilities, personality, etc. Write your thoughts below and consider adding them to your file folder.

> *Praise be to the Lord, to God our Savior, who daily bears our burdens.*
>
> *Psalm 68:19 NIV*

Continue to praise God by following up as a good steward of the opportunity to interview.

Write Your Thoughts...

Practice Interviewing

Before every interview, practice, practice, practice. First, answer each question by writing down talking points. Next, practice with a buddy or coach who asks the questions, and you answer with your workbook and talking points. Finally, you answer the questions without your workbook and talking points. Make sure to include relevant STAR stories.

Questions, Tips and Talking Points

1. Tell me about yourself.

Share your value statements, as well as relevant education, experiences, expertise and accomplishments. Because you researched the employer, job and interviewer, mention common background and interests. Talk no more than a minute or two.

2. Why do you want to work for us?

Focus on their needs and how you can meet them. Emphasize what you do and like best. Be positive. Convey an "I can do" attitude.

3. What do you find most attractive about the position?

Talk about the challenges and opportunity of the job. Share how your strengths can contribute to the success of the employer.

4. What are your strengths?

Give 3 work-related strengths. Share a STAR story that speaks to your strengths and success.

5. Tell me about your greatest accomplishment.

Give 3 work-related strengths. Share a STAR story that is most relevant to the employer's needs. Be enthusiastic. Keep your story to 1-2 minutes.

6. What salary/wages are you looking for?

Defer this question until later if possible. State that you are interested in overall opportunity to contribute and grow. If you must answer, share a range from minimum to target to ideal.

7. What are your career goals?

Relate your answer to the position for which you are interviewing. Talk about your desire to contribute to and grow with the employer.

8. Why should we hire you?

Share again your value statements, what you do best in light of what they seem to need most. Talk about how you can meet their needs through the job they want to be filled.

9. What are your weaknesses?

Be prepared to talk about a time when you failed to achieve your goals. Keep it brief. Do not elaborate unless asked. Tell what you have learned or have done to improve.

10. Can you tell us about a conflict you had at work?

If you say no or never had a conflict, some interviewers will dig deeper. Better to share even a small conflict and how you resolved it.

11. Why did you leave your last job or want to leave your current position?

If you are employed, talk about your goals and plans for meeting them. If you were laid off, fired or quit, share with them what you learned and how it will help you contribute in your next job. Do not say anything negative about current or past employers.

12. What do you know about our organization?

Share your research on the employer and the job. Share their mission, products, services, markets, size, scope. Tell them what you appreciate about them and the opportunity.

Find blank forms on our website at **crossroadscareer.org/interview**

Let's Talk Money

To have a conversation about money, you need to have at least started your compensation research.

Knowing your needs and wants for compensation can help you form a salary range that will assist you in your money conversations. Review your findings from Step 4, How to Target Opportunities, on page 50. If you are not sure how to calculate this range, a monthly spending plan can help.

> A monthly spending plan allows you to gather all your income and expenses into one place. Then use this simple formula, "Income - Expenses = Zero" allowing you to account for each dollar you earn, save, give and spend. This will provide the income range you need to pursue the right employment. To learn more, try Dave Ramsey's Financial Peace University or Compass books and resources.

From your monthly spending plan, write down the income range and benefits you need.

Salary & Benefits You Need

Do not start interviews by asking or talking about money. If the interviewer brings it up, you do not need to feel anxious, timid and/or uncomfortable. Conversations about salary and wage ranges, as well as benefits, are part of the mutual discovery process of whether a particular job is a good fit for you.

During the interview, do your best to focus on employer needs, what has to be accomplished, what you do best and how you can help them succeed. If possible, establish your value to the employer before discussing salary-wages-benefits.

During discussions about money, continue to build a personal relationship with employer representatives and emphasize how you can meet their needs. The more they get to know and like you, the more likely they will look for a way to hire you.

At the end of the first interview, ask about the salary or wage range of the position for which you are interviewing. If asked, share the minimum and preferred compensation you seek.

Three questions to ponder:

1. How does the compensation range work within your monthly spending plan?
2. How does this range compare with what similar jobs pay in your area?
3. What are other employers offering?

Employer flexibility on salary-wages varies dramatically depending on the size of the organization and level of the position. For larger employers with entry-level jobs, less flex. With smaller employers and/or more senior positions, sometimes more flex. Sometimes employers will pay more for contract workers doing the same job, but no benefits are offered.

The further you go into the interviewing process the more detailed conversations get about salary-wages-benefits. Use the Understand Offers Better in Step 7.

Be careful not to rule out a great employer because of a particular job's pay. If the job does not pay enough, ask if there may be some flexibility or perhaps other jobs that would be a better fit.

Get help with managing your money at *crossroadscareer.org/money*

Employment Tests

Be prepared for various tests and assessments as part of the interviewing-hiring process, such as…

- Personality and interest assessments
- Skills and cognitive tests
- Physical exams
- Drug testing

Being asked to take tests is good news. The day before and during assessments, eat right, exercise and get plenty of rest to be energetic and relaxed. For skills and cognitive tests, review whatever it is they are testing for. For personality and interest assessments, usually, your first answer is your best answer.

If you have results from other tests you have taken, and they show you are a good fit for their job, make a copy and share.

References

Reference requests are most appropriate after interviews have established a mutual interest between you and the employer.

Ask with whom they would like to speak. Be willing to share not only professional references who can speak to your abilities and accomplishments but also personal references who can talk about your character and passions. Be careful about giving a reference with your current employer. <u>Call or email people you give as references, so they are prepared for the employer to contact them</u>.

Background Checks

Before the hire is made, the employer is likely to ask for written permission to check your background. Checking may include work history, military service, educational degrees, professional certifications, criminal record, credit reports and more. If there is a problem in your background, be sure to share and explain it in advance.

Master Reference List

List name, relationship, email address, phone number and notes for everyone who could be a reference. For each job/employer you consider, pick references who are most relevant. Ask permission from each reference before giving their name. Double-check spelling and accuracy. Send references your resume so they can be prepared.

Name	Relationship	Email & Phone	Notes
Edward Example	Manager ABC Company	Edward@ABC.com 555-123-4567	Edward left ABC; now director at XYZ

Download a master reference list at **crossroadscareer.org/master-list**

Dress for Success

"Spiritual underwear" is more important than physical outerwear. Read the verses below and underline the words referring to armor.

Stand firm then, with the belt of truth buckled around your waist, with the breastplate of righteousness in place, and with your feet fitted with the readiness that comes from the gospel of peace…take up the shield of faith, with which you can extinguish all the flaming arrows of the evil one. Take the helmet of salvation and the sword of the Spirit, which is the word of God. Ephesians 6:14-17 NIV

Draw a picture of yourself wearing the full armor of God.

1. Belt
girded with truth

2. Breastplate
of righteousness

3. Shoes
gospel of peace

4. Shield
of faith

5. Helmet
of salvation

6. Sword
Word of God

How will the armor of God help you stand firm? _____

_____

Step Six Sorting

KEY TAKEAWAYS

What did you learn that was most important to you in this step?

STEP SEVEN
SELECTING

Trust in the Lord with all your heart and lean not on your own understanding; in all your ways submit to Him, and He will make your paths straight.

Proverbs 3:5-6 NIV

Walk In Good Works

God has prepared all of your steps. Trust and obey. Walk in His way in prayer. Believe in His word – a lamp for your feet and a light for your path.

An Offer Too Good to Refuse

Review again the Scriptural truth about walking through crossroads

For we are God's masterpiece. He has created us anew in Christ Jesus, so we can do the good things He planned for us long ago.
Ephesians 2:10 NLT

Be open to being hired as an employee, a self-employed contractor or even a business owner. Be flexible about compensation. Even when there is no money to be paid, you can still barter for food, clothing, shelter and services.

Prepare now and be alert. God may bring an opportunity at any time, sometimes when you least expect it.

How to Get an Offer

Invest 30 minutes to pray that God will help you be wise, as you make notes on the steps you have taken so far. Spend 5 minutes on each of these steps.

1. **Hear God Calling**
   Read through pages 15-16.

2. **Reach Forward**
   Refresh your attitude on pages 25-31.

3. **Discover Your Best**
   Review your gifts-passions-calling on page 44.

4. **Target Opportunities**
   Reconfirm key factors on page 52.

5. **Seek to Serve**
   Renew your praying, connecting and searching on pages 67-68 and 78-80.

6. **Wow Interviewers**
   Remember what employers appreciated about you on page 92.

7. **Walk in Good Works**
   Reflect on 6 steps above and summarize what you learned on page 106.

Reflect and Summarize

> ✏️ **Summarize what you learned from praying and making notes on previous page.**

> ✏️ **Write an email to the hiring manager and human resources representative/recruiter that represents your interest in the job and organization. Emphasize what value can you bring. Write your main points in the box below.**

While you are waiting for the employer to contact you after the interview, consider following up every week for up to seven weeks. You can email, send a postal note or call. Ideas for follow-up include:

- Express your interest and/or share another idea about how you can help.
- Check the news and their website for news/announcements to mention.
- Tell another relevant STAR story that you have not yet shared.
- If you get an offer from another employer.

How to Make an Offer

Rather than wait for an offer, consider taking initiative. Based on the job description and your interviews, write a one-page proposal to the hiring manager and human resources representative/recruiter that:

- Summarizes their needs.
- Lists the services, responsibilities and activities you offer.
- Outlines a work plan, timeline and cost.
- Explains the value and results they will get.
- Asks for phone or in-person appointment to talk through the proposal.

The work plan, timeline and cost outline can be offered as an independent contract worker or a W2 employee, and it covers:

- The number of hours per week you work.
- The number of weeks or months you work.
- The amount of money you are paid per hour, week, or month.

If you are proposing to work as an independent contractor, the per hour/week/month rate is usually higher than if you work as an employee. As a contractor, you will have to pay taxes, cover medical insurance and save for retirement on your own.

> *For example: If the job pays $50,000/year, which is equivalent to about $25/hour, then as an independent contractor you can ask for at least 50% more, or $37.50/hour, to cover taxes, insurance and retirement.*
>
> - It is not unusual to charge twice as much as a contractor versus being paid as an employee. In this case, $50/hour.
> - If you really like the employer and job opportunity, you can accept a contract position at $25/hour in hopes you will be hired as an employee later.

Not all employers are open to accepting offers for short-term and/or contract hiring, but most will appreciate you making the effort and offer.

How to Evaluate an Offer

If a verbal offer is made, listen attentively and respectfully. If you are not clear about any aspect of the offer, ask questions. Do not immediately debate or negotiate. It is best not to accept or decline the offer right away. Ask when an answer is needed. Tell them how appreciative and interested you are. Ask for the offer to be put in writing.

When you receive the offer in writing, read it carefully. Is there anything missing or unclear? Does it reflect what you were told? If you are not good with details, ask a trusted family member or friend to review it. Call or email the employer's key contact person with questions. If you have concerns or you need to negotiate, seek to meet in-person or at least talk by phone, instead of trading emails.

Evaluating an offer is not just about the job, pay and benefits, but also how you feel about the organization, employees, teamwork, boss and risk. Be sure you:

- Understand the title of the job, the reporting relationships, the hours per week required, the amount of travel if any.
- Get a feel for the culture, especially the personalities and values of key employees and management.

Questions you might find helpful include:

- What is the starting salary or wage? What is the total salary/wage range for the position? Any flexibility in the offer? How often are performance and salary/wage reviewed?
- Is there any commission or bonus? How much? Based on what? When is it paid? Is there a hiring bonus? Ask about reimbursement for the lost bonus you already earned but have not yet been paid from current employer?
- Is there insurance for health, dental, life, disability? Any portion of the cost for you and/or your family that you have to cover? How much?
- What about 401(k) and savings plans? Any deferred compensation or retirement plans? Do they offer stock or options in the company?
- How about the use of a mobile phone, laptop or tablet? Is there use of a car or a car allowance?

Understand Offers Better

When evaluating or making an offer, study each employer and job in light of your situation, needs and wants. The next three pages can help you analyze compensation, benefits and other key factors.

Name of potential employer

Name of the hiring manager

Position and Title

Responsibilities

Cash Compensation	Current-Recent	Offer	Needed	Wanted
Base Salary/Wage				
Bonuses				
Commission				
Overtime				
Other				
Total Cash Compensation				

Benefits	Current-Recent	Offer	Needed	Wanted
Health Insurance				
Dental Insurance				
Vision Insurance				
Life Insurance				
Disability Insurance				
Family Medical Insurance				

Benefits	Current-Recent	Offer	Needed	Wanted
Weeks of Vacation Per Year				
Number of Paid Holidays Per Year				
Number of Sick Days Per Year				
Severance Agreement				
Savings/ Retirement Plan				
Deferred Compensation Plan				
Stock/Equity Plan				
School Reimbursement				
Training/Development				
Financial Planning				
Office Equipment & Supplies				
Use of Auto/Pay Mileage				
Use of Phone/Service				
Use of Computer/Tablet				
Tech Support				

Benefits	Current-Recent	Offer	Needed	Wanted
Children Daycare				
Clothing Allowance/ Uniforms				
Paid Parking/Commuting				
Relocation Expenses				
Temporary Living/ Commuting				
Help with Spouse's Employment				
Cost of Living Adjustment				

Other Factors	Current-Recent	Offer	Needed	Wanted
Location and Travel				
Flexible Hours and Free Time				
Team vs. Individual Work				
High vs. Low Risk				

For more copies of this form, go to **crossroadscareer.org/offer**

Win-Win Negotiation

Not all employers are open to negotiation, but many are. Think of it as customizing the job not only for your benefit, but also for the benefit of the employer. Explore collaboration with the employer about how you can both get what you want and experience winning together.

Compare the first three common negotiation approaches to the better choice of collaboration.

NOT	NOT	NOT	BUT
They win, you lose	You win, they lose	Compromise, where each of you gets half	Collaborate for a win-win

Consider these steps to increase collaboration and a win-win by:

- Establishing your value first.
- Learning what things are most important to the employer.
- Highlighting results from what you do best that meets their needs.
- Doing your homework using salary/wage research tools.
- Knowing what you need in salary/wages and benefits.
- Discussing mutual interests, not positions.
- Focusing on WE, not just ME.

> In this example, identify problem areas for solutions:
>
> <u>Salary or wage is not high enough</u>. Perhaps the employer will let you work fewer hours for the same pay. Maybe you can be hired as a contractor with higher rates of pay versus working as an employee. Perhaps the employer can pay for parking expenses, commuting, use of a phone, etc. Look for compensation or benefits that cost them little, but the value would be great for you.

Not It?

How frustrating to be at Step 7, and the offer does not come or does not work!

One of our volunteers was looking for his next job after being laid off. On Friday, he had 10 opportunities developing, three of which looked like offers were coming. By noon the following Monday, all 10 were gone! He took a deep breath, learned from the experience and started over. The next job opportunity he got. It was so good that after a few years, he retired.

When you get a NOT IT, what you do next matters most. Consider these follow-up ideas:

- Explore with the employer whether "No" really means "No." Maybe it means "Not now." Might there be other jobs that would be a better fit?
- Keep the relationships you have made.
- Learn from the experience. What could you have done better or differently? See if you can get feedback from your interviews.
- If it is a door God closed, then say "Thank You!"
- Review Steps 1 and 2 about God's calling and your attitude.
- Always try to have two or more opportunities developing at the same time.

Got It!

Accept the final offer only if you believe it is work that God has prepared for you, you have received counsel from your close advisors, and there is agreement with your spouse.

As soon as you say "Yes," get and read a copy of our booklet, **New Job Jump Start** featuring 30 days with over 100 ways to get a great start in your new job.

Purchase New Job Jump Start at *crossroadscareer.org/store*

Thank Everyone

Make the time to send thank you notes by email and/or postal mail. Let them know the name of your new employer along with your new position, phone number and email. Appreciate how they helped you.

For those particulary helpful people, consider also sending a thank you note, a gift card or meaningful book. Perhaps you can treat them to a celebratory breakfast, lunch or dinner. Of course, offer to be of help if they ever need anything.

Help Others

Tell others about the 7-Step action plan you used to hear God calling, maximize your career and get the right job.

As you are walking through your own career crossing, you are uniquely equipped to help others. Share the blessings of what you have learned to encourage others.

> *Praise be to the God and Father of our Lord Jesus Christ, the Father of compassion and the God of all comfort, who comforts us in all our troubles, so that we can comfort those in any trouble with the comfort we ourselves receive from God.*
> *2 Corinthians 1:3-4 NIV*

Is God calling you to coach others, facilitate a small group or present at workshops? Would your church be interested in partnering with us? Connect with us today!

Prepare for Your Next Move

"What? I just got here!" you say. The last thing you want to think about is another move. However, the reality is that things can change fast.

Remember that the secret to your success is actually in the JOB:

J is for <u>joy</u>. — James 1:2-4
O is for <u>obedience</u>. — Ephesians 6:5-8
B is for doing your <u>best</u>. — Colossians 3:23-24

Be a good steward of whatever God gives you. Don't worry about what He does not give you, because you have no responsibility for what He does not give you.

Celebrate everyday that you are God's masterpiece.

With the speed of change combined with economic destruction and construction of whole occupations, industries and communities, you need to be prepared.

You are responsible for your career development and job search, stay alert and active every week by sharpening your skills, building your network, and serving others.

KEY TAKEAWAYS

What did you learn that was most important to you in this step?

Got questions or need help? Explore more Step 7 Resources online

crossroadscareer.org/step-7

Blessings to you for working through this workbook. Take a break and celebrate. Reward yourself, your mentor or buddy, or group with fun, fellowship and food.

You may or may not have found a new job or career, yet. Hopefully, you are making progress. Keep on keeping on!

For your next step, we recommend:

- Work through the **workbook & website** again with a buddy, coach, small group or in a workshop. Consider helping, leading or facilitating others.
- If you got a new job, read **New Job Jump Start**. You can study with a buddy or by yourself Day 1 through 30 or browse the contents for top hot topics every day.
- If you want to better hear God calling, get **Real Success at Work**, a 4-chapter individual or group study of Ephesians 2:10 about you as God's masterpiece.
- If you are interested in helping others, read through **Created for Good Works**, about the why, what and how you can help people hear God callling, maximize their career and get the right job.

Partner with Crossroads Career!

Is He leading you to share your time, talents and/or treasure to help others find purpose in their work lives? Perhaps you think your church, ministry, mission or school might want or need our help.

- Want to inquire about helping? Email **support@crossroadscareer.org**
- Interested to know more? See **crossroadscareer.org/about**
- Led to contribute financially? Go to **crossroadscareer.org/donate**

Footnotes

Page 2 At a Crossroads in Your Career?
- More than 150 million workers: US Bureau of Labor Statistics Civilian Labor Force 2019 https://www.bls.gov/news.release/empsit.a.htm.
- About half are dissatisfied: The Conference Board Job Satisfaction 2019 https://www.conference-board.org/press/pressdetail.cfm?pressid=9160
- Two-thirds are not engaged: Gallup Employee Engagement 2018 https://news.gallup.com/poll/241649/employee-engagement-rise.aspx

Page 12
What the whole world wants is a good job. *The Coming Jobs War* by Jim Clifton, Gallup Press ©2011

Page 13 Work as Worship
Face to Face Volume One. Praying the Scriptures for Intimate Worship, Zondervan Publishing House ©1997. Introduction Page X

Page 17 Career X Calling = Maximizing
Definition of "career" from www.dictionary.com
Definition of "call, called, calling" from www.studylight.info/vines

Page 18 Invest in You
Average length of unemployment from https://www.bls.gov/news.release/empsit.t12.htm

Page 25 As You Think, So You Shall Be
Abraham Lincoln quote: https://www.brainyquote.com/authors/abraham-lincoln-quotes
Zig Zigler quote from page 127 of "Over the Top" ©1994 Published by Zig Zigler Corporation

Page 28 Anger is One Letter Short of Danger
The Bondage Breaker ©1990 Neil T. Anderson Page 196

Page 30 Face the Fear
Freedom from Fear ©1999 Neil T Anderson and Rich Miller Page 204

Page 37 Love What You Do
If It ain't broke, BREAK IT! ©1992 Robert J. Kriegel and Louis Patler. Page 259

Page 45 You Are God's Masterpiece
Face to Face Volume One. Praying the Scriptures for Intimate Worship, Zondervan Publishing House ©1997. Introduction Page X

Page 70 Get Your Own Email
The ePolicy Institute quote from *Do's and Don'ts of Job Search from Work* https://www.thebalancecareers.com/job-search-from-work-do-s-and-don-ts-2062153

Pages 84-85 How to Wow Interviewers
All references to Wow Interview/Interviewers from Litton Group. See www.wowinterview.com.

Pages 109-111 Understand Offers Better
From Westerberg & Associates ©2012 see http://www.westerberginc.com/

Acknowledgements

The revitalized and expanded 2020 edition of the Crossroads Career Workbook and Website – You Are Created for Good Works – reflects the continuous input and feedback of more than 100 executives and experts in human resources, recruiting, career coaching, job searching, resume writing, training, development, education and ministry.

Special recognition and gratitude for our teammates:

Bill Ashby & Team, Printer and Owner of A&A Printing & Publishing
JJ Higgins, Creative Director and Owner of J. James Designs
Chris McGinn, Copy Editor

Thanks, too, for the support and guidance of our board of directors, partners in ministry, participating employers, and generous donors. For more than 30 years, Crossroads Career Services, Inc. has served over 50,000 people seeking to hear God calling, maximize their career and get the right job.

Most importantly, thanks and praise to God our Father and His Son Jesus Christ, who called us into this ministry of helping people through crossroads in their careers.

For more information, go to crossroadscareer.org/about.

More In Store For You
Visit *crossroadscareer.org/store*

New Job Jump Start
Great for individuals and employers

Getting a new job and getting a great start at that job are two different things. You want to have every possible advantage for success in your career. This is one of those great advantages – 30 days with over 100 ways to get a great start in your new job.

Real Success at Work
Super for individual study, with a buddy or in a group

Imagine getting up every day with the conviction that you are on the planet for a purpose. How fulfilled and fruitful would you be to know that you and your work matter to God and that He is pleased? How great would it be to experience real success? This study of Ephesians 2:10 helps you to discover how to hear and follow God's calling.

Created for Good Works
Fantastic reading for church and ministry leaders

If you want to help people find jobs, careers and God's calling, this is the book for you. When church members are unemployed, underemployed, or misemployed, it affects the life and vitality of the church. The solution is a spiritually vibrant yet practical career ministry helps people find jobs, careers and God's Calling. Learn the why, what and how to minister to people in their work lives.

Thousands of Jobs in Your Pocket
Get Our Phone App

Download our phone app for free. Search our Job Connector with thousands of employer-posted jobs, plus you can:

- Set up job alerts, apply for jobs, and track applications
- Create, keep, post and send resumes and cover letters
- Use the Interest Profiler and Skill Matcher assessments
- Connect to get counsel, contacts and encouragement
- Access our 7-step action plan, career and job resources
- Post, pray, and praise on our confidential Prayer Network

Hear God Calling | Maximize Your Career | Get the Right Job

Help others through crossroads

If you are interested in leading or hosting a group, class or workshop, or you know someone who could benefit from this workbook, you can order more today.

Order more workbooks at crossroadscareer.org/store